W9-AYE-631

Healing Fiction

James Hillman

Spring Publications, Inc. Woodstock, Connecticut

Copyright © 1983 James Hillman. All rights reserved.
No part of this book may be reproduced in any form or by any electronic or mechanical means including information storage and retrieval systems without permission in writing from the publisher, except by a reviewer who may quote brief passages in a review.

Published by Spring Publications, Inc., 299 East Quassett Rd., Woodstock, CT 06281. Printed in the United States of America. Third printing 1996. Cover designed and produced by Margot McLean and Slobodan Trajkovic. Text printed on acid free paper.

Distributed in the United States by the Continuum Publishing Group; in Canada by McClelland and Stewart; in the United Kingdom, Eire, and Europe by Airlift Book Co.; in Australia by Astam Books Pty Ltd; in Europe by Daimon Verlag; and in South Africa by Feffer and Simons

First published in 1983 by Stanton Hill Press, Barrytown, New York

"The Fiction of Case History: A Round" was written at the request of James B. Wiggins and published in a book he edited, *Religion as Story,* Harper & Row, Forum Book, 1975, pp. 123-73.

"The Pandaemonium of Images: C. G. Jung's Contribution to Know Thyself" was first presented at a conference at Notre Dame University (April, 1975), organized by Thomas Kapacinskas, in honor of the centennial of Jung's birth; it was first published in English in *New Lugano Review,* III, 3/4, pp. 35-45, 1977 and in German translation by the late Philipp Wolff-Windegg in *Eranos- Jahrbuch— 44,* 1975, edited by Adolf Portmann and Rudolf Ritsema, Leiden: Brill, 1977, pp. 415-52.

"Psychotherapy's Inferiority Complex" first appeared in Eranos-Jahrbuch—46, 1977, edited by Adolf Portmann and Rudolf Ritsema, Frankfurt a/M: Insel Verlag, 1981, pp. 121-74.

All three essays have been revised and expanded for book publication. I am glad to thank James Wiggins, Thomas Kapacinskas, the late James Fitzsimmons, the late Philipp Wolff-Windegg, and Rudolf Ritsema for their help in different ways with the original versions of these chapters and Michele Martin for help with the final version.

Library of Congress Cataloging-in-Publication Data will be found on the last page of this book before the ad.

Contents

1

The Fiction of Case History

The Fiction of Case History
A Round with Freud

1. The Fictional Freud

In 1934 Giovanni Papini[1] published a curious interview with Freud. It is presented as a straight-on dialogue, as if Freud were privately confessing just what his work was all about. This is what 'Freud' says:

> "Everybody thinks," [Freud] went on, "that I stand by the scientific character of my work and that my principal scope lies in curing mental maladies. This is a terrible error that has prevailed for years and that I have been unable to set right. I am a scientist by necessity, and not by vocation. I am really by nature an artist. . . . And of this there lies an irrefutable proof: which is that in all countries into which psychoanalysis has penetrated it has been better understood and applied by writers and artists than by doctors. My books, in fact, more resemble works of imagination than treatises on pathology. . . . I have been able to win my destiny in an indirect way, and have attained my dream: to remain a man of letters, though still in appearance a doctor. In all great men of science there is a leaven of fantasy, but no one proposes like me to translate the inspirations offered by the currents of modern literature into scientific theories. In psychoanalysis you may find fused together though changed into scientific jargon, the three greatest literary schools of the nineteenth century: Heine, Zola, and Mallarmé are united in me under the patronage of my old master, Goethe."[2]

The Freud in this interview reveals more of that master, and consequently of what psychotherapy is actually doing, than do the elaborations of Freudian theory. Psychoanalysis is a work of imaginative tellings in the realm of

3

poiesis, which means simply 'making,' and which I take to mean making by imagination into words. Our work more particularly belongs to the *rhetoric* of poiesis, by which I mean the persuasive power of imagining in words, an artfulness in speaking and hearing, writing and reading.

By placing depth psychology within a poetic and rhetorical cosmos, I am taking the consequences of a move I made in my 1972 Terry Lectures.[3] There I essayed a psychology of soul that is also a psychology of the imagination, one which takes its point of departure neither in brain physiology, structural linguistics, nor analyses of behavior, but in the processes of the imagination. That is: a psychology that assumes a poetic basis of mind. Any case history of that mind will have to be an imaginative expression of this poetic basis, an imaginative making, a poetic fiction, disguised, as Papini says, in the language of medical science, both by the teller in his tale and the hearer in his recording.

In the prefatory remarks to his famous 1905 publication, "Fragment of an Analysis of a Case of Hysteria"[4]—the Dora story—Freud writes: "I am aware that—in this town at least—there are many physicians who... choose to read a case history of this kind not as a contribution to the psychopathology of neuroses, but as a *roman à clef* designed for their private delectation." He also imagines "unauthorized," "nonmedical readers" turning to this story.

Already the 'reader' was figuring in Freud, the writer's, fantasy. And how often in his subsequent work we come upon these Victorian, these detective-story-style appeals to the reader, reminding him of what was said some pages back, or cautioning him that a point is worth holding in mind for it will appear again later, or showing concern for his wonder, confusion, perplexity—and maybe even shock at the bold frankness with which a matter is being exposed.

Freud's association to the elaborate disguised secrecy he employs in publishing the Dora case is not to sexual psychopathology (Krafft-Ebing had not felt this sort of concern for the reader or the cases), not to household medical advisors (Tissot published his dreadful warnings on masturbation with plenty of cases), not to forensic psychiatry, or to medical *Krankengeschichte* with their illustrations of naked ladies and gentlemen standing full front and white, masked only with black rectangles over the eyes (as if they can't see us, so we can't see them).

No. Freud's associations are with literature, for which he uses—always a sign of affective importance—a foreign term, *roman à clef*, meaning "a work which presents real persons and events, but disguised by the author." Now isn't this precisely what Freud did do, and so of course the nonmedical reader comes to his mind, because in his mind Freud was already associating himself with the writer of novels. The fantasy of the two kinds of readers—authorized and medical, unauthorized and literary—refer to two figures in Freud's own fantasy.

Why did Freud get himself into this tangle between the medical and the literary when trying to write psychological case reports? Was he not struggling with a form of writing for which there were no existing models? His mind moved back and forth between the two great traditions, science and humanities, an oscillation that had to occur—not merely because the medical was a cabalistic disguise for his literary vocation, finally recognized ironically by Papini, fraternally by Thomas Mann, and officially by his being awarded a Goethe prize for literature—but more likely the dilemma had to occur because Freud was in process of inventing a genre, the very vehicle that was to carry his new vision into the world. His psychoanalysis could make no further headway in the world of medicine, unless it could find a suitable form of 'telling' that gave the conviction, if not the substance, of medical empiricism. Freud tangled the two because he was engaged in both at once: fiction and case history; and ever since then in the history of our field, they are inseparable; our case histories are a way of writing fiction.

An analysis of "Dora," the first major psychological case history—the *Iliad* of our field—draws our attention to its literary technique even while it presents itself as a medical technique. By *technique* I mean "style as a deliberate procedure, craftsmanship,"[5] and I follow T.S. Eliot's notion of technique which shows the writer as a cool scientist rather than as a disheveled madman. And is it not just this literary question of technique, cool or disheveled, which distanced Freud from Stekel and Reich and Gross, drawing him closer instead to Abraham and Jones?

Technique also refers to formal values. Look at Freud's form in the case history of Dora. First the story as such. E. M. Forster[6] says: "The basis of a novel is a story, and a story is a narrative of events arranged in a time sequence"; we read on in a story in order to find out what happens next.

Simple primitive curiosity, says Forster. And Freud meets us on this level—suspense, hints, concealments, and a setting which evokes curiosity, the clinical consultation (part one of his case is called "The Clinical Picture"). There we are drawn in by another narrational technique, one we find in Joseph Conrad for instance: the incoherence of the story, needing the author (and the reader) to piece it together, and the two simultaneous levels on which it is being told by the main character (Dora).

Freud uses other devices: the modesty of the humble narrator in the background compared with the momentousness of what is revealed in his presence and to his reflection; the deepening of discoveries in answer to what happens next; the time limits pronounced at the outset, "only three months;" the enticement in the preface to forthcoming revelations of sexual details ("I will simply claim for myself the right of the gynecologist" with its pornographic echo of the young-girl-and-the-doctor); and then the sensitive apologies vis-à-vis the medical profession: no possibility of other specialists checking the results; not a verbatim report but written at the conclusion from memory; "the shortening produced by the omission of technique" (i.e., what he actually did in treating the case).

These apologies are of no small order! For just here, despite showing his awareness of the requirements of empiricism, our author begs off that method of writing in which he was thoroughly competent from his earlier work in brain pathology and cocaine experiments. A case history as empirical evidence in science would have to offer some means for public verification. It could not be merely a record from memory, unless it was to be taken only as anecdotal reminiscence: and the whole therapeutic technique employed—Freud's main omission—would have to belong to the record. We expect to learn exactly what the doctor did. Freud tells us only darkly and in part.

When setting out to show "the intimate structure of a neurotic disorder" (for that was his intention with this case), Freud could go either the way of Vesalius or of Balzac,[7] the anatomist or the moralist, the one revealing the intimate structures of physical morbidity, the other those of mental, moral, or psychlogical morbidity. He could approach the matter from the outside or the inside, or as the French writer Alain[8] puts it:

The human being has two sides, appropriate to history and fiction.
All that is observable in a man falls into the domain of history. But his

romanceful or romantic side (*roman* as fiction) includes "the pure passions, that is to say the dreams, joys, sorrows and self-communings which politeness or shame prevent him from mentioning"; and to express this side of human nature is one of the chief functions of the novel.

Where Alain speaks of politeness and shame, Freud writes: "Patients... keep back part... because they have not got over their feelings of timidity and shame."[9] Freud's histories are the stuff of fiction; they express the fictional side of human nature, its romance.

In the double dilemmas between history and fiction, between outside and inside, Freud prestidigitates the compromise that becomes his case style and our new genre of psychotherapeutic writing. He gives us the "pure passions... the dreams... the self-communings," but he does this from the outside as the medical pathologist of morbid structures, his first vocation. We do not enter into the inside of the case as we do in a novel, sympathizing with Dora, but remain outside, laying bare tissues, analyzing with Freud. As readers we identify with the main character, but not with her subjectivity, her feelings and torments. We identify rather with the "intimate structure of a neurotic disorder," the *idea* that the character embodies, sexual repression and its dynamisms. For the focus of our interest imperceptibly shifts from a subject being revealed to an object being exhibited, from the study of character to the analysis of character, and to a demonstration by means of character of the author's tendentious aims. (Thus he tells us less about her person than about her dreams, her material.) Our interest may be caught by what happens next and held by the author's subtleties of technique, but it is not the *story* that Freud is as much concerned with as it is the *plot*—and we shall come back to that.

Moreover, the action of the story—the discovery of the morbid factor and its process toward cure—has little to do with the character of the patient. The high drama of the action proceeds independently of her particular personality: Has she courage? Is she petty? What is the nature of her conscience? Where is her fatal flaw? What kind of moves is she likely to make in a crisis that will shape the course of the story? Despite its seeming intensity, the action of the analysis lies outside the character's influence upon it. The story could go on as well with anyone. Both patient and doctor could be replaced by another patient and another doctor in another town in another decade—and they are, for such is psychoanalysis as a scientific method. The case is merely an illustration, and so the character may not, cannot affect its action. It is not the character and the story, or the action, that reveals what is going on: it is the plot of psychodynamics. The characters are incidents of a universal plot and as such relatively incidental.

Compromise was Freud's formula for the nature of the dream, of the ego, of the symptom, and it was also the way he built his own dream theory as a compromising integration of the conflicting theories in the field at the time. [10] And because his case writing was a compromise we cannot follow either those who say Freud was "really a physician" with a fortunate literary gift, or "really a writer" who happened to appear in the field of medicine. The success of his style lies in the mask, that mask so necessary to the writer as Thomas Mann laboriously insisted, behind which the author must conceal himself in order that he may reveal himself.

His double movement is best put in his own terms. It is a compromise between an *unconscious* literary presentation (the style of the *romancier*) and the *conscious* analogy with physical medicine (the gynecologist simile). The manifest material was medical, but the latent intention, which necessitated the transfigurative suppression of medical, empirical methodology, was that of the poetic art. His case histories are brilliantly successful symptom formations, sublimated, transfigured into a new genre of narrative; they are like dreams: and all three—art, symptom formations, and dreams—are, in Freud's theory, compromises between two irreconcilable demands, providing defenses against awareness of what he was most deeply engaged in— fiction writing.

There are two other long case histories essential to the 'empirical foundations' of Freudian psychoanalysis—"The Phobia in a Five-Year-Old Boy" (1909) and "Comments on a Case of Paranoia" (1911). Like the first one, "Dora," these two have grown their more fictional titles, "Little Hans" and "The Schreber Case." [11] Here Freud leaves the requirements of case history as an empirical anamnesis and moves freely into his new genre. Here he has become an interpretive commentator, outside the scene of actual therapeutic operations. Freud did not analyze little Hans or Daniel Schreber. He analyzed the story told him by Hans' father and the story written in Schreber's memoirs.

We are not yet at that point in Freud's movement where he no longer needs to found his writing upon persons from his practice—or upon any practice at all. He essayed this style in three works: on Jensen's *Gradiva* (1907), on Leonardo (1910), and on Michelangelo's Moses (1914), the last published anonymously, with a deceptive editorial disguise. (The dates show these essays written parallel with his main case histories.) The *Gradiva* study is the analysis of wholly fictional dreams, dreams in a novel. But Freud's main ventures into the realm of wholly invented story are *Totem and Taboo* and *Moses and Monotheism*. These are religious fictions presenting Freud's science (in distinction to the scientific fictions presenting Jung's religion in his works on flying saucers, synchronicity, and alchemy). For *Totem and Taboo* and *Moses and Monotheism* no evidence can ever be empirically produced. Freud drops the empirical disguise and we see him as a writer of pure fictions. Ever since, we are all, in this field of psychotherapy, not medical empiricists, but workers in story.

2. *Theory and Plot*

Alain[12] gives another important clue to the nature of fiction: ". . . in the novel. . . everything is founded on human nature. . . everything is intentional, even passions and crime, even misery."

Plot reveals these human intentions. Plot shows how it all hangs together and makes sense. Only when a narrative receives inner coherence in terms of the depths of human nature do we have fiction, and for this fiction we have to have plot. Forster[13] explains plot like this:

> A plot is. . . a narrative of events, the emphasis falling on causality. "The king died and then the queen died," is a story. "The king died and then the queen died of grief," is a plot. A story answers what happened next; a plot tells us *why*.

To plot is to move from asking the question *and then what happened?* to the question *why did it happen?*

In our kind of fictions the plots are our theories. They are the ways in which we put the intentions of human nature together so that we can understand the *why* between the sequence of events in a story.

Telling us *why* is Freud's main aim with his case histories. All his narrative skills are assembled only for the sake of plot. Freud devised a plot that fits all his stories. Although the plot itself is simple enough, it requires complication, mystification, and fantasy. Freud's artfulness is necessitated by his theory. We have to have concealments and flashbacks to early reminiscences and screen memories. The plot has to thicken with the intense complications of transference and resistance, regressions in the development of character, and critical junctures in the forward thrust of the story. All this richness which results from the plot structure makes demands on our memory and intelligence—faculties which Forster says are essential to plots. And Freud's plot was absolutely economical: no loose ends. This economy in plot is called elegance in theory. Every Freudian narrative comes out the same way and can be taken apart to show one answer to the question *why*. The mystery is repression (in one of many varieties), followed by passions, crimes, and miseries (symptom formation), the involvement of the author (transference of the repressed), lifting of the repression through prolonged recognitions (psychotherapy), and the dénouement of ending therapy.

When Jung charges Freud with too simplistic a causal schema, he is faulting Freud for his plotting. Plots in human lives do not unfold side by side with one's story. The development of my life and the development of its plot are two distinct unfoldings. *Why* can be answered only by Freud in terms of time sequences, what happened first and what happened after that.

Why has still other answers than material and efficient causality: it asks also *what for* (final cause) and *why* in the sense of what archtetypal idea, myth, or person (formal cause) is at work in the story. Jung says we must look at the intentionality of the characters and where they are heading, for they are the main influence upon the shape of the stories. Each carries his own plot with him, writing his story, both backwards and forwards, as he individuates. Jung gives far more weight to individual character than either to narrative or to plot.

If "plot is emergent from the selective logic of the writerly act,"[14] then Jung considers Freud too selective and too logical, shaping all shoes on one last. Everything may be founded on human nature, but human nature itself is founded on things beyond human nature. Jung's plot (his theory of archetypes) is inherently multiplistic and variegated. Individuation shows many forms, has no prescribed momentum, and may come to no end.

Jung's cases pick up many colorful but extraneous threads. They don't make as thrilling reading as Freud's just because his plot has less selective logic and therefore less inevitability. Only when it is cast, or when we read it, in the model of a heroic quest or a pilgrim's progress does the individuation plot grip the reader. But that is only one archetypal mode of individuation, one mode of selective logic.

A reason that Alfred Adler's writings haven't the same fascination as Freud's is that Adlerian plot eliminates complexities. Adler's plotting—monistic like Freud's, one plot for all persons—does not allow as much secondary elaboration: symbolization, defenses, disguises, displacements, reaction formations, coded messages, and censoring. The main antagonists of the psychomachia (ego, id, superego) are done away with, so that much less demand is made upon the reader's intelligence and memory.

Freud presented his plot of human nature in the form of a theory, and this theory has its medical, biological, empirical language of libido. His double style of writing required that what was plot and myth on one level was theory and science on another. But for us who read him, it is important to bear in mind that our fundamental unease with Freud's theory is not that it cannot be verified but that it does not satisfy. We fail to fall for it not because it empirically fails as a hypothesis about human nature, but because it fails poetically, as a deep enough, embracing enough, aesthetic enough plot for providing dynamic coherence and meaning to the dispersed narratives of our lives.

Freud's one plot is named after a myth, Oedipus. With this move, Freud too placed mind on a poetic basis. He understood that the entire narrative of a human life, the characters that we are and the dreams we enter, are structured by the selective logic of a profound *mythos* in the psyche.

Freud's 'discovery' of the Oedipus tragedy located psychology at the very beginning of poetics, with Aristotle's use of *mythos* in his *Poetics*. When we open that book to read in English about plot, we find that wherever 'plot' appears the original Greek word is *mythos*. Plots are myths. The basic answers to *why* in a story are to be discovered in myths.

But a mythos is more than a theory and more than a plot. It is the tale of the interaction of humans and the divine. To be in a mythos is to be inescapably linked with divine powers, and moreover, to be in mimesis with them. Once Freud and Jung took the step into understanding human nature in terms of myth, they moved from human nature to the nature of religious powers. The poetic basis of mind suggests that the selective logic operating in the plots of our lives is the logic of mythos, mythology.

3. *The Empirical Fiction*

I am using *fiction* and suggesting that case histories are *fictions* in three senses of the word:

1. Case history as factual history, a true account or knowledge about the "succession of events through which anything passes"[15] is a fiction in the sense of a fabrication, a lie. But it is only a lie when it claims literal truth. Early on in the taking down of case histories, Freud found that he was not recording a true account of historical events, but fantasies of events as if they had actually happened. The material of a case history is not historical facts but psychological fantasies, the subjective stuff that is the proper domain of fiction in the sense of Alain and Forster above.

Case histories even today when we use tape recorders and public information from whole families still cannot claim that what is told in the tellings is a true account of the succession of events through which a thing has passed. This is supposedly so for history of any sort, and especially so for case history for these reasons: (a) case material must be solipsistic—about dreams, passions, fantasies, wishes, pains, none of which can be witnessed by the writer firsthand; (b) the material is particularly *fictive* (unbelievable, implausible) because it belongs to those surrealist and bizarre categories of events we clinically call hysterical, paranoid, hallucinatory, etc.; (c) external corroboration of a case history (by another clinician or a family member) is possible only in regard to limited circumstantialities; (d) anything referred to as 'history' must be yoked to chronicity, but psychic realities, as both Freud and Jung insisted, do not follow laws of time.

2. Case history is a fiction in the sense of an invented account of the imagined interior processes of a central character in a narrative story. Its writer is not the main character, that is, it is not autobiography; nor is it biography since the narrative events are severely selected by the demands of the plot. Essential to this fictional form is the empirical disguise.

Much could be said about empiricism in psychotherapy. I want only to touch it and only in one respect. One of the reasons for empiricism in philosophy, according to A.J. Ayer,[16] is "the egocentric predicament." Empiricism prevents solipsism; it gets us out of the circle of our minds by pointing to public, demonstrable events for corroboration. Empiricism is not only a defense against Platonism (innate ideas, universals, deductive idealism), it is, psychologically, that fantasy which makes us feel safe from solipsism, its isolation, its paranoid potentialities. Therefore, since psychological material is essentially subjective and the therapeutic situation a reinforcement by mirroring or doubling (the closed vessel) of this isolated subjectivity, the appeal to *the empiricism of therapy is a direct consequent of the solipsism of therapy.* The empirical disguise in case histories is an inevitable defence against the solipsistic power of the fictions with which therapy is engaged.

3. Case history, as the presentation of literal statements transposed to where they cannot be controverted or verified, is a fiction in the philosophical sense, i.e., a formula that must necessarily posit itself as beyond criteria of true or false, the as-if fictions of Vaihinger.[17] Here fictions are mental constructs, fantasies by means of which we fashion or 'fiction' (*fingere*) a life or a person into a case history.

We will be touching again upon these three kinds of fictions and their relevance for psychotherapy. But first we need to be impressed by the full actuality of this new kind of fiction, invented and developed during the twentieth century, written by thousands of hands in clinics and private practices and welfare centers, sometimes published but often not, mainly stored in the archives of asylums and the attics of analysts. At night, in the *Schreibstube* like Freud, the lonely therapist sits, recording, dictating, typing these accounts, in the grip of the stories of his patients and of their common therapeutic fantasy. All these stories, wherever and by whomever they are written, whether having a Freudian plot or a plot derived from any number of different myths, have one and the same leitmotif: *the main character enters therapy.* Therapy may appear as the dénouement (the classical anamnesis leading up to—"and that's why I came to see you, Doctor."). Or therapy may be the beginning of the story as Freud's cases which open with the character's arrival in the consulting room, e.g., the Rat Man case of 1909. Hence I call our genre *therapeutic fictions.*

As a detective story requires the discovery of the murderer, a heroic tragedy the death of the principal, and comedy a pleasing resolution of conflicts, so therapeutic fiction is the story of a person who comes to therapy, and, more often the story of the therapy than of the person. Therapy is either the whole content or the story which leads up to therapy. Roth's *Portnoy's Complaint* is therapeutic fiction in genre, even as it differs from it mainly in that Roth does not use the empirical disguise.

Usually therapy is the theme on which the narrative incidents are hung together, as the Dora story. Usually, too, therapy provides the means for focusing and selecting incidents, like a political novel choosing politically relevant events. And usually, the end of the story leads out of therapy into cure and world (or, for an antitherapeutic dénouement, a 'failed case'). Freud concludes his Dora story with these words: "Years had gone by since her visit. In the meantime the girl has married... and been reclaimed once more by the realities of life." As the tales of this genre are written with a therapeutic eye, they are read with that same eye by a new genre of reader, who can, in fact, read even Shakespeare, Faulkner, or his own biography as pieces of therapeutic fiction. How this has come about in Freud we have seen. Now, what does it imply?

4. Stories in Therapy

The sophisticated 'therapeutic class' who come to private therapy have their stories already formed into the therapeutic genre, that is, the story is self-reflective and focused upon the 'problems' of the main character. With the 'hospital population' the shape of the story often requires coaching from the listener: there are too many main characters (projections); incidents are not selected according to the economical requirements of a therapeutic plot; time sequence, basic to the definition of narrative, may be altogether missing. Although the listener shapes the tale into the therapeutic genre, the condition of the teller—that which makes him a hospital patient—plays a large part in the form of the tale, especially its stylistics.

Patients use their stories in different ways. Some tell stories as entertainments to while, or wile, away the hour, others are reporters, others are prosecuting attorneys building a plaint. Occasionally a tale becomes wholly metaphorical in which every aspect of what-I-saw-yesterday—the large building site, the hard-hatted foreman in a control booth, the little girl in a shiny silver rain puddle in danger from a bulldozer, the passerby who intervenes—all refer as well to figures within the patient's psyche and their interplay.

A clinician is supposed to note the way stories are told. Old textbooks of psychiatry, such as Eugen Bleuler's, referred to style for aid in diagnosis. The psychiatrist was encouraged to note florid expansiveness, rambling, alliterations, punnings and bizarre word associations, hyperbole, archaicisms, mannerisms—terms we may find in literary textbooks on style. A diagnosis is partly made on the basis of a person's style of telling his tale.

A psychological diagnosis too is a 'telling about the patient.' It is a caricature, an abbreviated character sketch—Szasz and Goffman might say 'character assassination'—in the language of a clinical specialist to be read by other clinical specialists. (It's definitely not for the patient.) A psychological diagnosis does not say what a person has, or what a person is. It describes his *Zustandsbild*, his clinical picture. It tells about the presentation of self to the clinical writer.

The clinical writer tells one into a diagnosis, into an 'abnormal story.' I mean abnormal in two ways: first it is a story written with an eye for the morbid, deviant, and bizarre—like a Gothic novel or a tale by Poe, presented with the naturalism of Zola. But, unlike a Gothic novel, a tale by Poe or Zola—and this is the second meaning of abnormal—this story takes itself literally, believes itself as factual history and thus deviates from the norms of a story. Diagnoses are wholly literalistic in their historicism—and of course it is wholly necessary that they be told in this way in order to organize the character about whom they are written into precisely the style of fiction that the writer is empowered to create. Diagnoses are highly creative acts of writing. The force of their literalistic stories is overwhelming (as are all literalistic writings where imagining is disguised as the truthful mirror of 'real facts'). Literalism is anyway the main instrument of the clinical mind.

The force of diagnostic stories cannot be exaggerated. Once one has been written into a particular clinical fantasy with its expectations, its typicalities, its character traits, and the rich vocabulary it offers for recognizing oneself, one then begins to recapitulate one's life into the shape of the story. One's past too is retold and finds a new internal coherence, even inevitability, through this abnormal story. A diagnosis is indeed a *gnosis*: a mode of self-knowledge that creates a cosmos in its image.

In each case the story leads into therapy, as we said. And this also means that I the therapist-writer have now entered the tale, in fact, become a key figure in a story whose beginnings, development, plot, and style have had, until this meeting, nothing to do with me. I have never known, and probably will never know, any of the other characters, take part in any of its other scenes, or be apprised of what happens next or what clinics call the 'follow-up.'

Yet, there was no story in the therapeutic genre until 'I' got into it, so that from the moment the person crosses the threshold into therapy a whole new story begins—or rather, the former story has an entirely new slant as the original tale is re-visioned into the therapeutic genre. Here begins that difficulty called resistance, that attempt by the patient to forget, distort, conceal in order to retain the first version. Here begins too that other difficulty called counter-transference, the therapist-writer's self-indulgence in the story.

Two authors are now collaborating in a mutual fiction of therapy, though conventionally only one of them will write it. Both are so grabbed by the story, become internal objects of it, that their collaboration can become a *folie à deux* which shows the power of plot over the will of the characters.

A colleague once told me about a new patient walking out on her when she challenged the thematic mode of the patient's story. The patient presented himself as a rather sick case, having been more or less steadily in therapy for fifteen of his thirty-six years; things had not much changed (alcohol, homosexuality, depressions, money worries), and he had tried many kinds of therapy. My colleague said: "For me, you are a new case, and I don't accept that you are as sick as you believe you are. Let's begin today." By refusing his web of constructions, she also cut him off from his supporting fiction. He did not return. His story still made sense to him: an incurable, but still a dues-paying member of the therapeutic traffic. He wanted analysis and the analyst to fit into his story.

A second case, this one from my practice: psychotic episodes, hospitalizations with medical abuses, seductions, and violations of rights, shock treatments and 'helpful drugs.' I took this story like a past another woman might tell of: falling in love in high school and marrying the boy next door, having a loving husband, children, and a spaniel, a story of making it. In other words both are consistent accounts exposing a thematic motif which organizes events into experience. Both of these women, this one from her percale sheets and the other from her canvas strait jacket—to put the fantasy figuratively—might come in to therapy, desperate, saying precisely the same thing: "It doesn't make any sense; I've wasted the best years of my life, I don't know where I am, or who I am." The senselessness derives from a breakdown in the thematic motif: it no longer holds events together and gives them sense, it no longer provides the mode of experiencing. The patient is in search of a new story, or of reconnecting with her old one.

I believed her story to be her sustaining fiction, but that she had not read it for its hermetic possibilities, its covert meanings. She had taken her story literally in the clinical language in which it had been told her, a tale of sickness, abuse, wastage of the best years. The story needed to be doctored, not her: it needed reimagining. So I put her years of wastage into another fiction: she knew the psyche because she had been immersed in its depths. Hospital had been her finishing school, her initiation rites, her religious confirmation, her rape, and her apprenticeship with psychological realities. Her pedigree to survival and diploma was her soul's endurance through, and masochistic enjoyment of, these psychological horrors. She was indeed a victim, not of her history but of the story in which she had put her history.

You will have noticed that my colleague contested a story of sickness and I confirmed one, but that both of us clashed with the presenting fiction, thereby beginning the battle of stories which is an essential aspect of face-to-face therapy and of clinical case conferences. We saw this already in Freud with Dora. He took her story and gave it a new plot, a Freudian plot: and part of this plot is that it is good for you; its the best plot because it cures, which is the best dénouement of the therapeutic genre.

The talk going on in depth analysis is not merely the analysis of one person's story by the other, and whatever else is going on in a therapy session—ritual, suggestion, eros, power, projection—it is also a contest between singers, reenacting one of the oldest kinds of cultural enjoyments that we humans know. This is partly why therapy pretends to being creative, and I use that word advisedly to mean originating of significative imaginative patterns, poiesis. Succcessful therapy is thus a collaboration between fictions, a revisioning of the story into a more intelligent, more imaginative plot, which also means the sense of mythos in all the parts of the story.

Unfortunately we therapists are not aware enough that we are singers. We miss a lot of what we could be doing. Our ways of narration are limited to four kinds: epic, comic, detective, social realism. We take what comes—no matter how passionate and erotic, how tragic and noble, how freakish and arbitrary—and turn it all into one of our four modes. First, there are the cases showing the ego's development, especially out of childhood, through obstacles and defeats: heroic epic. Second, the tales of tangles, the confused identities and uncertain genders, the impossible bumbling inadequacies of the foolish victim, but which come out with a happy end of adjustment: comic. Third, unmasking hidden plots through clues and crises, indefatigably tracking down what went wrong by a taciturn but twinkle-eyed, pipe-puffing detective, not too unlike Holmes or Poirot. Fourth, the detailed descriptions of small circumstances, true to life, the family as a misfortune, environmental conditions as another, all presented with lugubrious sociological terminology and the heavy-handed panned shots of tendentious importance: social realism.

Psychology would do better to turn directly to literature rather than to use it unawares. Literature has been friendly to us, openly incorporating a good deal from psychoanalysis. Those in literature see the psychology in fiction. It's our turn to see the fiction in psychology. [18]

For instance, we might look at the picaresque mode. Its central figure does not develop (or deteriorate), but goes through episodic, discontinuous movements. His narrative ends abruptly without achievement for there is no goal so the dénouement can neither be the resolution of comedy nor the fatal flaw of tragedy. Rather than using such large programmed scales, success and failure is measured by the flavor of daily experiences. (There is precise attention paid to eating, dressing, money, sex.) There are tales within tales that do not further a plot, showing that psychic history goes on in many places at once—meanwhile, back on the farm, in another part of the forest—and in many figures at once. Other personages of the story are as interesting as the main character, just as the other figures within our dreams and fantasies often bear more upon our fates than does the ego. There are no lasting relationships, and much emphasis upon personae, the garbs and masks of life at all levels, especially the shadow world of pimps, thieves, bastards, charlatans, and pompous dignitaries. These figures, in us each, are the realm of picaresque reflection, of seeing through every established stance, yet without moral implication. And though the picaresque character suffers defeat, depression, and betrayal, he does not progress by means of suffering into light.

From the tragic perspective such a way of framing a case history is a waste; soul demands something more metaphysically important. From the comic viewpoint there would have to be a resolution, some sort of accepting awareness and adaptation to the society which to the picaresque person is always hostile. From the heroic standpoint, the picaresque mode is a psychopathic parody of the individuation epic—but then individuation might be a paranoid organization of the picaresque. The same tale told as social realism would turn into a political tract, as indeed anarchism and the picaresque thrive best in Spanish soil.

But I have made my exhibition: case histories have different fictional styles and may be written in a variety of fictional genres. And therapy may be most helpful when a person is able to place his life within this variety, like the polytheistic pantheon, without having to choose one against the others. For even while one part of me knows the soul goes to death in tragedy, another is living a picaresque fantasy, and a third engaged in the heroic comedy of improvement.

5. Genre and Archetype

A Jungian friend, Wolfgang Giegerich, while exposing the archetypal pattern within the writings of Erich Neumann, makes the remark:

> Something (some 'factor') obviously keeps us from the truly psychological orientation and makes our thinking unpsychological by making us wish for, or even need, empirical verification, scientific truth, and systematizations. This 'factor' is our containment in the Great Mother/Hero myth, whose nature is to create the (mythic!) fantasy of the possibility of heroically breaking out of myth, into 'fact,' 'truth,' 'science.'[19]

He then develops the theme, showing that a narrative account in evolutional terms is a genre which belongs to the perspective of the Hero/Great Mother. This implies that when we conceive our life story as a Battle for

Deliverance from the Great Mother—as Jung called it—we are engaged in heroics; these heroics reflect in such concepts as ego development, ego strength and personal identity. The theory emerging from this archetypal perspective is that of Neumann's *Origins and History of Consciousness*. That book is not a statement of *faith* in progress or a work of *science* in evolution. Nor is it, as Giegerich shows, a *history* in any other sense of that word but story. It is rather an archetypal fantasy held together by a captivating plot: the development of Ego, an Everyman, with whom we each can identify. Its persuasiveness rests upon this same archetypal foundation—the rhetoric of the archetype—which in this example casts each of us readers into an ontogenetic recapitulation of the heroic battle of deliverance from maternal uroboric claustrophobia.

Giegerich links a genre of psychoanalytical writing with an archetype. In a short paper of my own I also tried to show that a certain style of presenting psychology, Jung's in particular, by means of diagrams, numbers, and crystals, by references to introversion and slow patience, and by images of the Old Wise Man, uses of ancient wisdom and magic, belongs to the senex consciousness of Saturn. [20] Again, the rhetoric of an archetype. Again, a genre which determines our plots and our styles in writing case history.

The relationship between archetype and genre has been worked out most famously by Northrop Frye in his *Anatomy of Criticism*, where the four classical genres of literature are each given a season in the year, so that literature follows a cycle of the corn god. Actually Frye's system, though fourfold, remains still within the single myth of the Great Mother, the God-Hero her son, and the cycle of nature.

More fundamental than any of these attempts at the problem of genre and archetype, is an approach that can be extrapolated from a paper by Patricia Berry. She considers that narrative as such cannot help but reflect the ego's concerns, because narrative is essentially the genre of the hero archetype. She writes:

> Narration is also reinforced by therapy. As we tell our dreams, so we narrate our life stories. Not only the content of our dreams is influenced by analysis but the very style of our remembering. . . . Since the narrative style of description is inextricably bound with a sense of continuity—what in psychotherapy we call the ego—misuse

of continuity because of the ego is also close at hand. ... The most important difficulty with narrative: it tends to become the ego's trip. The hero has a way of finding himself in the midst of any story. He can turn anything into a parable of a way to make it and stay on top. The continuity in a story becomes *his* ongoing heroic movement. Hence when we read a dream as narrative there is nothing more ego-natural than to take the sequence of movement as a progression culminating in the dreamer's just reward or defeat. The way story encapsulates one into it as protagonist corrupts the dream into a mirror in which the ego sees only its concerns. [21]

A similar thought has been put succinctly in Roger Fowler's dictionary: "The narrative without a hero remains a critical fiction."[22] Even the antihero is what we in psychology would refer to as a negative inflation of the ego. Whether invoked or not, ego is always present. If we are going to tell tales in narrative form we are going to come out with ego theory. Berry implies that the genre of narrative itself determines the plot by which we form our case history and understand it.

The question now arises: is our style of case-history writing, even of interpreting individual dreams and situations, the result of ego psychology, *or* is it possible that ego psychology—as presented first by Freud, then by one division of his school, and now by the therapeutic establishment— results from our style of case-history writing? Have we produced ego psychology through our way of writing cases? And are our case histories not so much empirical demonstrations of the way the psyche works but empirical demonstrations of the way that *poiesis* works in organizing our vision?

This means we would begin to read case histories with an archetypal eye toward their form. We would be interested in the genre in which the case is fantasied, even the rhythm, the language, the sentence structures, the metaphors, for we find archetypes not only in the content of a case history: form too is archetypal. There is an archetypal psychology of form. Thus we would open ourselves to the idea that were the story written in another way, by another hand, from another perspective, it would sound different and therefore *be a different story*. I am suggesting the poetic basis of therapy, of biography, of our very lives.

Perhaps the examples of the heroic ego and the picaresque are not enough to show what I mean. Let us return to the abstractions of senex consciousness where we move away from narrative altogether, both epic and episodic.

We find in this senex style of case writing, both Freudian and Jungian, an emphasis upon reductions, either downward to castration anxiety, omnipotence fantasy, primal scene, etc., or upward to wholeness, self, fourfoldedness. The work of analysis is presented less in terms of what happened next than in terms of descriptive states of being, basic abstractions of powers at work in the soul. The abstractions and reductions can be theoretical in terms of libido and its quantifications, or historical, numerical (quaternio), or configurative (mandala). The images of a dream, instead of being primary and irreducible as Jung's own theory itself states, become representations of something more abstract. The lady in the shop window repairing carpets is not that precise image and its metaphorical implications, but is a representation of a nonrepresentational and abstract mother image to which it can be reduced. The scenes of childhood are not taken either as images, or linked into developmental narrative, but become exemplars of theoretical universals, anal or Oedipal. Events do not tell a story but expose a structure. This stucture is then applied to other events across time and to images regardless of context—attempts to be best in school, obsession with changing underwear, fear of the dark forest in camp —uniting them together as manifestations of the one root principle.

No longer is it a question of what happened next and how did one move through this situation into the next one. Rather it is a question of instances exemplifying principles, images as allegories, scenes as enactments in time of eternal verities. In this genre of examining a case—and I say examining deliberately—the function of consciousness, represented by the writer-analyst, is that of seeing abstractions, a keen-sighted perspicacity into structures and laws.

Here the connecting function of consciousness is defined, not hermetically in terms of significances, or martially in terms of activation, or erotically or Dionysianally, but systematically, through a paranoid ability to see defenses and resistances as mechanisms (not as obstacles in the heroic course of progression). Finally, the dénouement in this genre is less in terms of a goal in the patient (improvement, say), which belongs to the narrative style and to ego development, than it is an instruction in the science of analysis, a contribution to theory, adding another stone to its monument. Saturn, the senex.[23]

You will have noticed that I threw in a few alternatives that we have not yet discussed: hermetic writing where connections do not close up but open and reveal; Aphroditic where the eye is on sensate value, personal relatings, perhaps, or sex; Dionysian where flow matters most. I also have left only as a hint the point of view of the anima which, as I see it, would stay with images and fantasies themselves, never translating them or organizing them into narrative or through plot, but responding to them in a metaphorical style where consciousness is one of innuendo, reflection, echo, tone, and elusive movements.

The idea that there is a God in our tellings and that this God shapes the words into the very syntax of a genre is not new in literary studies even if it might come as a shock to my colleagues who really believe they are only writing clinical accounts of facts. Annabel Patterson,[24] for instance, has taken up again "The Seven Capital Stars" or description of the seven ideas of style employed in Renaissance compositions. There we see how different Gods can be linked with genres, i.e., gravity with Saturn, speed with Mercury, beauty with Venus, vehemence with Mars, and the like. Of course, these one-to-one parallels should not be forced: polytheistic psychology can't speak straight on, one-to-one. Rather, they are to be imagined as suggestive perspectives towards writing and reading clinical accounts and towards listening to the language of the patient.

My point in this section has already been made in that same article by Berry: "The way we tell our story is the way we form our therapy." The way we imagine our lives is the way we are going to go on living our lives. For the manner in which we tell ourselves about what is going on is the genre through which events become experiences. There are no bare events, plain facts, simple data—or rather this too is an archetypal fantasy: the simplistics of brute (or dead) nature.

Rhetoric means the art of persuasion. And the rhetoric of the archetype is the way each God persuades us to believe in the myth that is the plot in our case history. But the myth and the God are not something set apart, to be revealed in numinous moments of revelation, by oracle, or through epiphanies of images. They are in the rhetoric itself, in the way we use words to persuade ourselves about ourselves, how we tell what happened next and answer the question *why*. To find the Gods in psychology we ought to look first at the genres of our case-history writing.

Our reflection needs to turn to psychoanalytic literature as *literature*. I am suggesting that literary reflection is a primary mode of grasping where one is ignorant, unconscious, blind in regard to the case because one has not differentiated the subjective factor, the Gods in one's work.

6. *Soul History vs. Case History*

Before we go any further we need to come back to a distinction made above by Alain between history as stories of outer events and fiction as stories of inner events. This same distinction was crucial to my argument in *Suicide and the Soul* where I held that suicide can be understood, if at all, only from the viewpoint of soul and its inner history. Outer events of the case record are not enough. Let me repeat what was said there:

> Outside and inside, life and soul, appear as parallels in 'case history' and 'soul history.' A case history is a biography of historical events in which one took part: family, school, work, illness, war, love. The soul history often neglects entirely some or many of these events, and spontaneously invents fictions and 'inscapes' without major outer correlations. The biography of the soul concerns experience. It seems not to follow the one-way direction of the flow of time, and it is reported best by emotions, dreams, and fantasies. . . . The experiences arising from major dreams, crises, and insights give definition to the personality. They too have 'names' and 'dates' like the outer events of case history; they are like boundary-stones which mark out one's own individual ground. These marks can be less denied than can the outer facts of life, for nationality, marriage, religion, occupation, and even one's own name can all be altered. . . . Case history reports on the achievements and failures of life with the world of facts. But the soul has neither achieved nor failed in the same way. . . . The soul imagines and plays—and play is not chronicled by report. What remains of the years of our childhood play that could be set down in a case history? . . . Where a case history presents a sequence of facts leading to diagnosis, soul history shows rather a concentric helter-skelter pointing always beyond itself. . . . We cannot get a soul history through a case history. [25]

The subsequent softening of this radicality takes more pages than can be reprinted here, but nonetheless the distinction remains sharp. Case history is brushed aside as "the achievements and failures of life with a world of facts." It is merely a relic of the medical model, incidental to the concerns of the soul.

But this won't do. What about case history, not only as a written document but as an actuality of each existence? We each have our stories—parents and schools, sicknesses and diplomas, jobs held and loves lost. Are these so trivial and accessory to the soul? The struggle with case history in this paper carries on from that work on suicide: what *does* case history tell us? Why have it at all?

As long as the problem is locked into the old mechanical dualities of soul and world, inner and outer, psychological and medical, we chug on down the same old ruts. Instead we have to see the inner necessity of historical events, out there, in the events themselves, where 'inner' no longer means private and owned by a self or a soul or an ego, where inner is not a literalized place inside a subject, but the subjectivity in events and that attitude which interiorizes those events, goes into them in search of psychological depths.

The core mistake of mechanism in psychology is that it literalizes functions and actions as discrete moving parts, separated from each other. The core mistake of my two sorts of 'histories' was this mechanistic separation of soul and case, the latter further becoming wholly hardened into literal facts. The passage above puts that strongly enough. By being so tough-minded about case history as hard facts, I could free soul history to be wholly inner, important, and symbolic.

That model of two histories embraces the mistake that historians are supposedly aware of, the mistake of historical literalism, that what is written in a history is what actually happened, a report of the facts, a verifiable account of actual events as they actually were. Alain too makes this mistake, placing history all on one side and fiction all on the other. This separation ennobles case history with literal reality which then must be equaled by overemphasizing—as I did above—that soul history has the same sort of reality: "they too have 'names' and 'dates'... like boundary stones...." Having literalized the outer, I had to literalize and harden the inner.

What I missed there and want to correct here is that a case history—no matter how 'outer' its style—is also a mode of imagining. I would take case history anew, as one of the ways the soul speaks about itself, as a case and with a history. Then we can respect case history for the mode of fiction that it is: a fiction cast in literalisms which necessarily does not recognize itself as such, because, as we shall work out in this round, this kind of literalism is necessary to the soul. It wants its literal case history, adding to it as it engages in life.

Above all we cannot claim inner certainties of the soul against the flux of outer facts. What we tell ourselves about our 'true' entities and landmarks of the soul are as subject to dissolution, misapprehension, and shifting boundaries as are any 'outer' events. We can be as deluded about ourselves as about the world's facts. The distinction between a case history of outer events and a soul history of inner experiences cannot be made in terms of indelible permanence and literal truth. Neither is more 'real' because it is more solid. We have to affirm psychic reality in another way—not by copying the literalistic metaphors, the fantasies of fixity and hardness, that we use for outer reality.

To make the distinction between inner and outer on other grounds, means seeing the movement between soul and history to be a process that is continually internalizing and externalizing, gaining insight and losing it, deliteralizing and reliteralizing. Soul and history are names we give to this more fundamental operation going on between what Hindu thought refers to as *suksma* (subtle) and *sthula* (gross), between the fictional metaphorical viewpoint and the literalistic historical viewpoint, between inwardness and outwardness. It is not that there are two kinds of events, or two places of events, but two perspectives toward events, an inner psychological one and an outer historical one.

Now we come to a fundamental in the relation between soul and history. An event becomes an experience, moves from outer to inner, is made into soul, when it goes through a psychological process, when it is worked upon by the soul in any of several ways. Plato gave us main ones: dialectic, certain kinds of mania including love and ritual, and poetry, to which we can add sickness or pathologizing as the thanatological activity of the psyche. We can take in the world by putting it through sickness; by symptom-making we can turn an event into an experience. But a simple narrative, just a story, is not enough to make soul.

A love story is but an *histoire*, one of *mille e tre*, only the outer history of emotional events, like a crowd of yellow daffodils, unless it be recollected in tranquility, put through a psychological operation, such as the soul itself compels to—love letters, anxieties, poems, confidences, hazardous assignations, tumescent fantasies. Dreams, visions, and feelings—so entirely inner and mine—have nothing to do with soul unless they be recollected, recorded, entered into history. Inner images and feelings (so-called soul-stuff) are free for grabs, nightly at the oneiric fair, simply giveaways from the tunnel of love and the chamber of horrors unless they be put through the qualifying intelligence, the history-making of the psyche, sifted and weighed in the disciplined reflection of loving, of ritual, of dialectics, of an art—or of a psychological analysis with its therapeutic plot.

You see that here I am speaking of history as an equivalent for soul-making, as a digestive operation.

These two ways of history reappear in the opposition between soul and case. The case kind of history is the story of outwardness, raw gross matter, unfermented, undigested, unworked. And this case material (as it is just as well called) can be equally the intense private fantasies of an LSD trip or a religious epiphany, or dull public papers from my files—so long as this material has not been worked over and ingested to become experience. Outer means simply we are outside looking at it; it is closed in its factual literalism. This and this happened, and then this. Inner means we are taking it in; it is open to insight. Ingestion slows down the happenings for the sake of the chewing.

We can regard history from the viewpoint of soul. By carefully collating what happened, history digests events, moving them from case material to subtle matter.

Hidden in this fantasy is a tenet of my faith: soul slows the parade of history; digestion tames appetite; experience coagulates events. I believe that had we more experiencing there would be need for fewer events and the quick passage of time would find a stop. And then I believe that what we do not digest is laid out somewhere else, into others, the political world, the dreams, the body's symptoms, becoming literal and outer (and called historical) because it is too hard for us, too opaque, to break open and to insight.

What we do not experience becomes only case material or world history, hastening the pace of events both in my soul and in the world. All haste comes from the devil, as an old saying goes, which psychologically means that one's devil is to be found in one's indigestion, in having more events than are experienced. What we do experience by putting events through an imaginative process is taken off the streets of time and out of the ignorant sea of my mental turbulence. We beat the devil by simply standing still.

Or going backwards—regression belongs to the digestive mode of soul-making, so that a good deal of remembering, its pain, its shame, is recapitulation, revising the chapter again before it can close. Analysts probably ought to re-write their cases as often as novelists their fictions. Writing up the case, then re-writing and editing, belong to its therapy, healing the fiction of its ill-considered moments, its undigested remnants. We too need to purge our writing of the fashionable jargon of borrowed ideas, conventionalism, and self-reflecting conceits. We need to notice adjectives, prepositional phrases, even commas, that make for precision and sharpen the images to essentials. As we analysts become more literate, we may become less literal, stuck in the case without a vision of its soul. After all, psychotherapy means a therapy of psyche and its practice may not be limited only to the person who has passed through the clinic to disappear anonymously in life. The follow-up in writing is our digestion. The practice goes on in the practitioner, and we are still 'practicing' with the cases of Freud. Psychotherapy advances only by regression, going back over the material one more time, re-writing its own history.

For this reason I worship psychologically at the altar of the God of historical time and slowness, Saturn, the archetypal swallower, who teaches us the art of internal digestion through the syndrome of his magistral depressions.

It is curious to find that analysis does not regard history in this beneficial manner. Deep psychotherapies go into a person's past with the desire of altering that past, even shedding it. A person is a case with a history *because* of history. Therapy is a kind of *opus contra historiam*. It works against the historical influences of childhood and society in order to uncover a true ahistorical self and free it. So we find deep therapies invoking ahistorical principles, such as instincts, timelessness of the unconscious, rebirth, archetypes, and other eternal universalities such as the Oedipus complex or the self. *Deep* tends to mean beyond or outside of history. These therapies also try to give the soul a history that is independent of its case material, a soul whose history recapitulates phylogeny or religious individuation.

But I come at this history question from another angle. I see the opposition between the two kinds of history as a necessity of the therapeutic plot. Therapy requires the fiction of literal realities as the primary material to work on. It must have the raw in order to cook. So we begin with a classical anamnesis. But this move is not in order to be grounded in facts, but because these factual stories are the primal matter in which the psyche of the patient is stuck. He is immersed in these literal attachments and identifications, the clinging circumstantialities of *physis*. Here is the apparently soulless abyss, the unformed, unpsychological material full of sibling data, economic figures, passage through welfare centers, aches and pains and needs, not yet 'worked up' into a plot: it's all prior to fermentation.

This level of the fiction must present itself literalistically. The therapeutic plot needs opaque events in order to make insights. What is more, the therapeutic plot as a continuing process continues to need new materials in order to go on making soul. So a case history and its material run along contiguous with soul history and make soul history possible. Therapy profits from keeping the borders between 'outer' and 'inner' in order to move things back and forth between them with its art of interpretation.

Interpretations require well-kept borders—perhaps even make those borders. Perhaps, all those carefully defined borders that encompass therapy— between patient and doctor, between objective and subjective, symbols and concepts, conscious and unconscious—derive from therapy's first, basic move of interpretative translation. Defenses, resistances, opposites, ego-boundaries: this is a language of the border. Perhaps, transference itself is a function of interpretation; and were we to let go the borders requiring translation between two languages, we wouldn't have the tense transference between the two people.

Suppose that instead of imagining borders as ditches and trenches between opposing sides, requiring censors, interpreters, professional rules, we imagine them as mirrors. Analysis as mimesis. Then therapy evokes corresponding images, back and forth. The image which the patient brings receives an imaginative reflection from my side, rather than a translation into my language. We respond to paintings and music without translation, why not as well the dream? Imaginative art forfeits interpretation and calls instead for a comparable act of imagination. Your dream evokes a dream in me, mine in you—not literally as such, not mutual sharing and confession (which loses the image in personal subjectivism)— but dream as reveries, fantasy, imaginative response, a piece of soul-making whose aim is not hermeneutic, not a gesture of understanding. Along the mirrored border one does not hear the language of meaning; understanding each other is not the aim and so translation falls away. There is instead a miming dance back and forth of the border guards, the greetings of images, exchange of gifts, ceremonies.

Have you glimpsed toward whom I am pointing? Hermes. He is God of borders and hermeneutics, of connections between sorts of worlds. As a procedure of interpretation, psychotherapy has invited in wily, mercurial Hermes, with his commerce, his phallus, his deceits, who then must be brought under control with restriction which, as borders, only encourages Hermes ever more strongly. A vicious circle, the hermeneutic circle. Endless analysis because ever more unconscious material for conscious interpretation.

My point here is not that Hermes is the wrong God for analysis. My point is that once he has been invited in, then we better know what we might expect. He is himself a healing fiction, a God. And Hermes heals by convincing us of that fiction of interpretation, making it work, so that the interpreter hits just on the word which opens the way. But if Hermes is to function properly as guide of souls we must have some material for him to turn into a message. No dreams—no therapeutic insights. There must be something to move across the threshold and exchange, translate into an insight. He appears in the interpretive act; his gift is the insight. One recognizes where he has been by the mound of stones erected to mark his intervention. And these boundary stones go on being erected in the psyche as part of its soul history (as mentioned above) after a bit of deft hermeneutical work has been done on a dream or a story.

When Hermes is at work in an analysis, one feels that one's story has been stolen and turned into something else. (My woman colleague who 'cheated' her new patient by not giving him what he wanted for his story: that was a Hermes move, even if it didn't work.) The patient tells his tale, and suddenly its plot has been transformed. He resists, as one would try to stop a thief. . . this is not what I meant at all, not at all. But too late: Hermes has caught the tale, turned its feet around, made black into white, given it wings. And the tale is gone from the upperworld historical nexus in which it had begun and been subverted into an underground meaning.

Freud and Jung each began with these hermetic tricks. "Something crazy happened to me yesterday" became for them hermeneutic messages. They took the slips of the tongue, jokes, and the oddities of word associations right out of their innocent *prima facie* context and into the vast caverns of psychic significance. They were both masters of hermetic conversion, turning case material into soul.

7. Jung: Child of Hermes?

Besides the genres we have pointed to—hermetic, heroic, picaresque or episodic, erotic, Saturnian, and that of the anima—we can find the seeds for another in Jung. [26] But we must look in the right place. For, although Jung made several contributions to the relations between psychology and litera-ture (*CW* 15), these belong among the more conventional depth psycho-logical approaches to the subject. They are general, and they put the whole matter in terms of opposites: personal/collective unconscious, aes-thetic/psychological, creativity/normality, form/content, etc. Jung's scarce observations on fiction, with the exception of his piece on Joyce's *Ulysses* and his affinity with Goethe's *Faust*, refer in the large to second-rate writers like Rider Haggard. His real contribution, like Freud's, is in the fictions he himself constructed, his very way of writing psychology. *Answer to Job* is the most evident of these, but even more interesting analogies to literary productions are his phenomenologies of different archetypes— trickster, Mercurius, child, anima, mother—which are the creative inven-tion of fictional personalities, biographies or character descriptions of archetypal persons.

Like Freud's, much of Jung's published case material (excluding his early psychiatric and Freudian papers, i.e., work done before age thirty-seven when Jung became what we now call Jungian) is a giant step removed from clinical empiricism. When he refers to cases, as he does all through his written works, it is not in the clinical empirical sense, but as anecdotal fillers, or as instances of a point. His cases are secondary illustrations often prefaced with the remark: "I would like to illustrate this by an example."[27]

Though "an analysis of a prelude to a case of schizophrenia," as he subtitled *Symbols of Transformation* (*CW* 5), Jung's most famous long case, "Miss Miller," is, like Freud's Schreber case, an analysis of a printed document, originally written by an American, the French translation of which Jung worked through in German. His second most important published case (*Psychology and Alchemy* [*CW* 12]), like Freud's Hans, was material from a patient who did not work analytically with Jung. Jung expressly chose a case not his in order that the demonstration of his theory by means of the case be yet more objectively empirical, i.e., less subject to his influence (cf. *CW* 11, §38). Even that notorious Burghölzli patient, upon whose spontaneous fantasy of the solar-phallus creating wind became the 'empirical' base of Jung's hypotheses of the collective unconscious and the archetypes, turns out to have been not his own case, but that of his pupil Honegger who told Jung about it.[28]

When Jung introduces the one volume of his collected works embracing his papers on empirical analysis and empirically entitled *The Practice of Psychotherapy* (*CW* 16), he says: "This book may serve to give the reader a good idea of the empirical foundations of psychotherapy." The pedestrian reader expects 'case material,' but the eleven cases mentioned in the book—except for the short posthumous one appended by the editors in the second edition after Jung's death—are *en passant* anecdotal references, or are patients' *dreams* serving as material for Jung's method of interpretation.

The way in which the later Jung uses 'empirical' is worth a study in itself for he refreshes a term that has shrunk into an encrusted cliché of scientism. I think that his use of the word refers to a subjective process in himself and is more in keeping with the poet's use of empirical. The empirical event— the solar-phallus image in a patient—releases a movement in the mind setting off a hypothesis (or an image, a line of verse). One then points to the empirical event as the efficient cause, for indeed the hypothesis did start up from an empirical fact with a time and a place, as a poem may start in a concrete perception. And, like the poet, Jung returns ever and again to the concrete world of perceptions (cases, dreams, religious fantasies, ancient texts). In this first sense he is empirical. He is, second, empirical in accumulating instances to support his hypotheses, and, third, in the pragmatist sense of evaluating hypotheses in terms of practical therapeutic heuristics. But he is not empirical, not even in the clinical sense of the single case as paradigm, because the case is not the indispensable source of his insights or the place of their proving.

Except—the case of his autobiography. This came at the end of his twenty-volume cosmology and was not intended to belong to the evidence for his much earlier theories, although it subsequently turns out to have been the main empirical vessel of his entire work.[29] For Jung's work, like Freud's theory of dreams, repression, and the unconscious, results from one principal case history and is demonstrated by it, the author's own.

In sum, Jung's presentation of cases is decidedly not medical empirics— reports on the interactions between physician, patient, pathology, and treatment—but rather his case material presents spontaneous psychic fictions and their interpretations. (The relation of these dreams and fantasies to the 'case' and to the doctor [Jung] is barely sketched and usually incidental.) His cases are also not anamneses, biographical presentations of life, a mode he expressly abjures:

> The accusation has been made in certain quarters that the newer psychotherapy is concerned too much with philosophical problems and not enough with the minutiae of case-histories. This accusation must be emphatically rebutted, because philosophical problems belong in the highest degree to any empirical study of the psyche, as fit subjects both for research and for philosophical criticism. The empirical intellect, occupying itself with the minutiae of case-histories, involuntarily imports its own philosophical premises not only into the arrangement but also into the judgement of the material, and even into the apparently objective presentation of the data. If psychotherapists today are beginning to talk about a *Weltanschauung*, a philosophy of life, this merely proves that they have discovered the existence of certain broad assumptions which were formerly overlooked in the most ingenuous manner. What is the use of even the most accurate and punctilious work if it is prejudiced by an unavowed assumption?[30]

So what are we left with? The interpretation of and commentary upon spontaneous psychic imaginings. The stuff is fiction though it be called 'unconscious material.' Where Freud was a writer of fictions, in the sense above, Jung is a writer on fictions. And, for Jung, the more fictitious and far-out the better (hence, alchemy, Tibet, Zarathustra, astrological aeons, schizophrenia, parapsycholgy) for such 'materials' obliged him to meet them on an equally imaginative level. But—both Freud and Jung assumed an empirical posture, subjected themselves to empirical criticisms, and attempted to reply with empirical defenses. They would have been better served had they turned for help to the field in which they were themselves working, the field of the literary imagination.

Jung's style of writing psychology takes various forms, sometimes exhortative and apocalyptic as a heretical preacher, sometimes with the charts and figures of a Wundtian experimentalist, sometimes with the whacky systems, impenetrable language, and arcane references of an early Gnostic from the Near East. Like Hermes whose winged feet touch down as well in Hades as on Olympus and who carries messages from every one of the Gods, Jung's hermeneutic knew no barriers of time or space—Chinese yoga, Mexican rites, contemporary historical events, hospital patients, modern physics—he would interpret anything; anything was *prima materia* for his psycholgical operations. His psychology presents itself as a continuing essay, *Versuch*. No more than any other great essayist, Montaigne or Emerson for instance, Jung, too, as he always insisted, did not write a system. That his second generation of followers quickly showed the buried cosmology within the unsystematic essays—complete with maps and figures—still does not make Jung himself any less hermetic. The one work (volume 7 of the *Collected Works*) which did 'essay' a systematic approach, was written originally before his main works on science, religion, myths, alchemy, and psychic reality had even been conceived. (That this book is still used as primer to Jung's work shows how desperate we are for explanatory *systems* of psychology and not insightful *essays* into it.)

So Jung's way of writing psychology seems to have been under the tutelage of Hermes in several ways: the concern for borderline conditions of the psyche; the engagement with psyche's hermetic secrets; and, third, his hermeneutical research along the borders of psychology, where odd fields touch each other. Moreover, Jung's work is a hermeneutic itself in a Hermes style. It does not create a new cosmology but resignifies this one by guiding it toward psyche and psyche toward death. All things bear messages for the soul from the Gods. Hermes appears in Jung's concern with the myth of meanings, his attraction ever and again to Mercurius, whether in schizophrenia, synchronicity, transformation, death, or in the hermetic art, alchemy. Hermes also is the trickster who can twist a word, like 'empirical,' to carry the message needed at the moment, so as to slip another meaning through. In the center of his Bollingen stone-carving surrounded by the glyphs of the planets is the sign of Mercury.[31] Mercury among other things, is the God of writing.

But in my own mercurial way the God I want to point to in Jung is not Hermes, but Dionysos, and in order to do this we must turn to Jung's discussion of the dream.

8. *Dream, Drama, Dionysos*

Jung did not accept Freud's fiction of the dream; it was both too contrived and too simplistic. For Jung the dream was not allegorical—"a narrative description of a subject under guise of another,"[32] in which "characters, actions and scenery are systematically symbolic."[33] The dream was metaphorical, speaking two tongues at once, or, as he put this hermetic duplicity, the dream is a symbol, a throwing together of two dissonants into a unique voice. The difference between Freud and Jung is the difference between allegory and metaphor. And the difference between allegory and metaphor is more profoundly determinant of the true schools of psychology and the understanding of the soul and its speech than are differences derived from the plots, or theories, of Freud and Jung.

Allegory and metaphor both start off saying one thing as if it were another. But where the allegorical method divides this double talk into two constituents—latent and manifest—and requires *translation* of manifest into latent, the metaphorical method keeps the two voices together, hearing the dream as it tells itself, ambiguously evocative and concretely precise at each and every instant. Metaphors are not subject to interpretative translation without breaking up their peculiar unity. The man has a wooden leg is no longer a metaphor if one says: see, under his trousers, one of his legs is artificial; or if one takes the other tack, saying: I mean only figuratively that his style is similar to one with a wooden leg. It is fake, hollow; it limps, drags. Since symbols and metaphors cannot be translated, another method for understanding dreams is needed, a method in which masks, disguises, and doubleness inherently belong, a method that is itself metaphorical.

This metaphorical mode of speech is for Jung the voice of nature itself; Jung's favorite metaphor for the dream was that it was nature itself speaking. By this he meant, at least to me, both *natura naturans* (the primordial force of nature) and *natura naturata* (the primordial forms of nature, the ambiguous but precise archetypal images). By turning to dreams for the creative nature in the soul, Jung was also turning to the God of this nature, Dionysos. He is both the life force, *zoe,* and the ambiguous flow of primordial fantasy; he is always a child, bisexual, and the Lord of Souls, the psychic life of transformation through half-hidden events. Jung pointed to Dionysos also by stating that the dream had a dramatic structure. Dionysos is the god of theater: the word *tragedy* means his "goat song."

When Jung said the dream had a dramatic structure and its nature could be read as theater, he made the same sort of move as Freud. Both projected onto the dream the idea by which they were viewing the dream. Freud said the dream contained repressed sexuality, whereas he was viewing it and deciphering it by means of that idea (which, by the way, is not just an instinct theory or a biological model but an archetypal plot expressing Aphrodite, Eros, Priapos, and Dionysos-Liber). Jung said the dream had dramatic structure, whereas he was using the perspective of drama to read the dream. This confusion between what we see and how we see is another example of the effect of ideas. An *eidos* means originally that which one sees and that by which one sees. Actually we can see the dramatic structure only if we see by means of it. We see what our ideas, governed by archetypes, allow us to see.

Jung's step into drama was another of his literary moves. Again he took a crucial step approximating psychology to poetics. Moreover (to put this thought as a hypothesis, and in italics for staggering your mind): *if the dream is psychic nature per se, unconditioned, spontaneous, primary, and this psychic nature can show a dramatic structure, then the nature of the mind is poetic.* To go to the root of human ontology, its truth, essence, and nature, one must move in the fictional mode and use poetic tools. To understand the structure of dreaming we turn to drama; poesis is the via regia to the via regia. The unconscious produces dramas, poetic fictions; it is a theater.

In a work (CW 8) not published until 1945, Jung lays out the four stages of dramatic structure: Statement of Place, Dramatis Personae, Exposition; Development of Plot; Culmination or Crisis; Solution or Lysis. I won't repeat it here; you will enjoy reading it for yourself. It is instructive, useful —and misleading. For the dramatic structure is not true on the level Jung posits it: the dreams one sees in practice can rarely be analysed into four clear-cut stages, because dreams are mainly abrupt and fragmentary or hysterically swollen and meanderingly long. Moreover, the notion of dramatic structure is misleading in a deeper sense: the dream is primarily an image—*oneiros* (dream in Greek) means "image" and not "story" (cf. Berry, *op. cit.* on the relation between narrative and image in dreams). We may see the dream narratively, allegorically, or dramatically, but it is itself an image or group of images. When we see drama in it, we are always, in part, seeing our own hypothesis.

The Dionysian hypothesis has been valuable for seeing the *dream* in another way; it will be even more valuable for seeing *Dionysos* in another way.

Dionysos has been written off, or adulated, for his hysteria. He has come to mean simply the opposite of Apollo, [34] and has thus become in the popular, and scholarly mind too, a creature of raving maenads, communal ecstasy, lost boundaries, revolution, and theatrics. Logos has to be brought in from elsewhere, e. g., Apollo. But when Jung says the dream has a dramatic *structure* he is saying it has a dramatic *logic*, that there is a Dionysian logos and this is the logic of theater. The dream is not only psychic nature; it also presents psychic logic. (Freud of course presented the first grammar of this logic in part seven of his *Traumdeutung*. But that work can also be seen as a perverse turning of poetic rhetoric into patholog-ical mechanisms. The terms Freud uses for the dream work—condensation, displacement, symbolization, and the like—are the very ways of poetic diction.)

I believe what Jung is suggesting is this: if psychotherapy is to under-stand the dreaming soul from within, it had best turn to 'theatrical logic.' The nature of mind as it presents itself most immediately has a specific form: Dionysian form. Dionysos may be the force that through the green fuse drives the flower, but this force is not dumb. It has an internal organi-zation. In psychology this language speaks not genetically, not biochemi-cally in the information of DNA codes, but directly in Dionysos's own art form, theatrical poetics. This means the dream is not a coded message at all, but a display, a *Schau*, in which the dreamer himself plays a part or is in the audience, and thus always involved. No wonder that Aristotle placed psychotherapy (catharsis) in the context of theater. Our lives are the enactment of our dreams; our case histories are from the very beginning, archetypally, dramas; we are masks (*personae*) through which the Gods sound (*personare*). Like dreams, inner fantasy too (to which we turn more closely in Chapter Two) has the compelling logic of theatre. Jung writes (*CW* 14:§706):

> A chain of fantasy ideas develops and gradually takes on a dramatic character: the passive process becomes an action. At first it consists of projected figures, and these images are observed like scenes in a theatre. In other words, you dream with open eyes. As a rule there is a marked tendency simply to enjoy this interior entertainment.... What is enacted on the stage still remains a background process; it does not move the observer in any way, and the less it moves him, the smaller will be the cathartic effect of this private theatre. The piece that is being played does not want merely to be watched impartially, it wants to compel his participation. If the observer understands that his own drama is being performed on this inner stage, he cannot remain indifferent to the plot and its dénouement. He will notice, as the actors appear one by one and the plot thickens, that... he is being addressed by the unconscious, and that *it* causes these fantasy images to appear before him. He therefore feels compelled, or is encouraged by his analyst, to take part in the play.

This startling literary analogy to the healing process takes us back to Greece and the place of Dionysian theatre in healing. The patient moves into the role of enacted one, actor. Healing begins when we move out of the audience and onto the stage of the psyche, become characters in a fiction (even the God-like voice of Truth, a fiction), and as the drama intensifies, the catharsis occurs; we are purged from attachments to literal destinies, find freedom in playing parts, partial, dismembered, Dionysian, never *being* whole but *participating in* the whole that is a play, remembered by it as actor of it. And the task set by the play and its God is to play a part with craft, sensitively.

To put dreams with drama and Dionysos means not to put them with prophesy and Apollo. Jung's move invalidates the entire oracular approach to the dream, an approach Jung himself often fell for, reading the dream as a prophetic message of what and how to behave: dream interpretation as counseling for daily life. Again: not messages; masks.

If the structure of Dionysian logic is drama, the particular embodiment of Dionysian logic is the actor; Dionysian logos is the enactment of fiction, oneself an as-if being whose reality comes wholly from imagination and the belief it imposes. The actor is and is not, a person and a persona, divided and undivided—as Dionysos was called. The self divided is precisely where the self is authentically located—contrary to Laing. Authenticity is the perpetual dismemberment of being and not-being a self, a being that is always in many parts, like a dream with a full cast. We all have identity crises because a single identity is a delusion of the monotheistic mind that would defeat Dionysos at all costs. We all have dispersed consciousness through all our body parts, wandering wombs; we are all hysterics. Authenticity is *in* the illusion, playing it, seeing through it from within as we play it, like an actor who sees through his mask and can only see in this way.

Failure to understand this Dionysian logic, that our dramas are filled with form and dynamic coherence because they are plotted by myths in which the Gods participate, drives one outside. We attempt to see through what is going on from the viewpoint of the detached observer. Then we have Pentheus up his tree, the schizoid Apollonic movement out of hysteria, depriving logic of its life and life of its logic. Both are mad.

The essence of theater is knowing it is theater, that one is playing, enacting, miming in a reality that is completely a fiction. So, when Dionysos is called Lord of Souls it means not only the metaphysical sense of death and the mysteries of the underworld. It means also Lord of psychic insight, the psychological viewpoint which sees all things as masks in order to see through all things. For where masking is essential to a logic, then seeing through is implied. Dionysian logic is necessarily mystical and transformational because it takes events as masks, requiring the process of esotericism, of seeing through to the next insight. It is his logic that necessitates his attributes of movement, dance, and flow. His is the viewpoint which can take nothing as it is statically, nothing literalistically, because everything has been put literarily into dramatic fictions. All the world's a stage, we are such stuff as dreams are made of, said Elizabeth's court psychologist.

We have been long led to believe that logos can be defined only by Olympian structures, by children of Zeus and Athene, or by Apollo or Hermes or Saturn—logos as form, as law, as system or mathematics. But Heraclitus said it was a flow like fire; and Jesus that it was like love. Each God has its logos, which has no single definition but is basically the insighting power of mind to create a cosmos and give sense to it. It is an old word for our worst word, consciousness.

Dionysian consciousness understands the conflicts in our stories through dramatic tensions and not through conceptual opposites; we are composed of agonies not polarities. Dionysian consciousness is the mode of making sense of our lives and worlds through awareness of mimesis, recognizing that our entire case history is an enactment, "either for tragedy, comedy, history, pastoral, pastoral-comical, historical-pastoral, tragical-historical, tragical-comical-pastoral,"[35] and that to be 'psychological' means to see myself in the masks of this particular fiction that is my fate to enact.

Finally, to view ourselves from within a drama refers to the religious origins, not only of drama, but of the mythical enactments that we perform and name with the mask of 'behavior.'

9. The Need to Historicize

Freud's crucial discovery that the stories he was being told were psychological happenings dressed as history and experienced as remembered events was the first recognition in modern psychology of psychic reality independent of other realities. It was, further, a recognition of the independence of memory from history and history from memory. There is history that is not remembered—forgetting, distortion, denial, repressing; there is also memory that is not historical—screen memories, confabulations, and those tales told him of early sexual trauma and primal scenes that had not occurred in the literal historical past.

The separability of history and memory—that memory is not a reliable guide to history and can falsify it—is old hat to historians. Hence their insistence upon objective documentary evidence. No document, no event. But that history is not the very substance of memory, that memory originates, presenting its productions as reproductions, throws open wide windows to a view of the mind, to reminiscence, and to the sense of time.

Platonists find nothing startling in Freud's rediscovery of what they had always said. From the *Meno*, through Augustine's *Confessions*, the Art of Memory in Guilio Camillo, to Swedenborg, Romantic philosophy, and Rudolf Steiner, *reminiscence* is never only of facts that happened in your or my lifetime, imprinted on the wax tablet of the mind, stored and retrieved through links of association. Memory for Platonism is a vast potential of all knowledge written not merely by the hand of events but by the signature of the Gods; all images and the mental activity that summons them is in some direct but obscure relation with the mind of God. To reminisce in the Platonist sense was to move right through history into gnosis.

To be correct, this remembering-what-never-happened must rightly be called imagining, and this sort of memory is imagination. *Memoria* was the old term for both. It referred to an activity and a place that today we call variously memory, imagination and the unconscious.[36] *Memoria* was described as a great hall, a storehouse, a theatre packed with images. And the only difference between remembering and imagining was that memory images were those to which a sense of time had been added, that curious conviction that they had once happened.

Cut free from having-to-have-happened, from the need to be historical, memories become pre-historical images, that is, archetypal. The events called forth from the storehouse of *memoria* are mythical in the Platonist sense of never having happened yet which always are.[37] They are eternally present—not forgotten, not past; they are present now, just as Freud rediscovered them at work in the present psychopathology of everyday life.

The way into these memorial halls is personal; we each have our own doorways which make us believe that *memoria* itself is personal, our very own. The psychoanalytical couch is one such door; the poet's notebook, the writer's table are others. Yet the *memorability* of specific images—the little neighbor girl in a yellow sunsuit digging to China on the July beach; the lost bloodied tooth in the party cake—that precisely these images, and these images so precisely, have been selected, retrieved, recounted tells that their vital stuff is archetypally memorable. Memory infuses images with memorability, making the images more 'real' to us by adding to them the sense of the time past, giving them historical reality. But the historical reality is only a cover for soul significance, only a way of adapting the archetypal sense of mystery and importance to a consciousness engrossed in historical facts. If the image doesn't come as history, we might not take it for real.

Remembering is thus a commemoration, a ritual recall of our lives to the images in the background of the soul. By remembering, we give a kind of commemorative legend, a founding image to our present lives, just as in Freud's cases their memories provided the legendary background for their present therapy and for the founding of psychoanalysis. The sexual traumata did indeed 'happen'—but in the imagination—and are always happening as ritual commemorations, as founding legends on which the Freudian institution, and its dogma, its cult, its priesthood have been established.

I need to remember my stories not because I need to find out about myself but because I need to found myself in a story I can hold to be 'mine.' I also fear these stories because through them I can be found out, my imaginal foundations exposed. Repression is built into each story as the fear of the story itself, the fear of the closeness of the Gods in the myths which found me. Thus the art of therapy requires a skillful handling of memory, of case history, so that it can truly found the patient. Hence the importance of introducing the great myths into therapy. They are ways of reading personal history in the foundational mode of fiction.

Since Freud, the stuff of psychotherapy has been memories. If, however, this stuff is actually commemorative legends, then psychotherapy has actually been engaged in mythopoiesis, like the other arts. The father of therapy may be Freud, but its mother is Mnemosyne, *Memoria*, mother of the muses, whose tenth, invisible, daughter must be Psyche.

Psychotherapy first set out to heal memory. The first step in that treatment occurred when Freud cured memory of its notion of itself as history— Mnemosyne's identification with one particular daughter, Clio. The second step cures memory of its fixation on its remembrances by recognizing them as images. Memory heals into imagination. The final step takes place as we recognize that memory, remembering, goes on through her daughters, in modes of musing, in imagining, so that psychotherapy encourages the musing, that activity which frees memories into images. As we muse over a memory, it becomes an image, shedding its literal historical facticity, slipping its causal chains, and opening into the stuff of which art is made. The art of healing is healing into art. Of course, not literally. . . .

We have come to this point having taken off from Freud's crucial discovery that the productions of memoria presented themselves in his cases as reproductions of history. Why does the psyche need to present experience dressed in the costumes of the past, as if it were history? Why does the psyche historicize?[38] What does historicizing do for the soul?

This seems to me the most important psychological question arising from Freud's insight into the historical 'falsification' of memories. For this 'falsification' is nothing other than the historicizing activity of the psyche itself. The psyche itself makes 'history' that is altogether fictional. We are not merely making history, but making it up as we go along. Henry Corbin always insisted history is in the soul (not we are in history). History-making is a musing, poetic process of Clio, proceeding as an autonomous, archetypal activity, presenting us with tales as if they were facts. And we cannot transcend history, not because we cannot get out of time or escape the past, but because we are always in the soul and subject to its musings. Historical necessity is not historical determinism—caught in history's objective traces, dragged along. Historical necessity means rather we are caught in our stories, the soul's histories, tragedies, comedies, its need to form its subjectivity as history.

It has been argued, and I confess to having once taken this line, that placing events in the past is a defensive maneuver. It shows split feelings: one cannot stand for a shame and so one puts it into the past tense. When I say: I used to lie to my former analyst; I used to masturbate; I used to hear voices, but no longer, not now—this puts distance between myself and the action. By placing the scandal in the past, it no longer presses me so closely. I disown it. Historicizing is a cover-up.

But I now regard these moves into history to be means of detachment. To call them defenses returns us to the ego who is accused of not taking stands, of splitting, of not owning up. But not the ego makes these moves, the psyche does. It spontaneously historicizes, even in dreams, and it does this, I believe, to gain a particular kind of distance as a means of *separating an act from actuality*. Lying, masturbating, hallucinating become psychic events not ego events, something for reflection rather than for control. They are now less affective and personal, more collective and general, part of a story rather than a report. Because they have been disowned, they have moved from true confession into historical fiction where they can be looked at in another light.

In this sense the cover-up of history is for the sake of discretion, maintaining an event intact but removed, in a glass vessel so that it can be puzzled over without being identified with. It remains my crime, but the crime is no longer me. I can move about it, whereas were it happening here and now I would be at its mercy, without insight, only recriminations and defenses. The move into past tense in analysis signals that the psyche wants analysis. The move is an attempt at self-healing, enclosing the wounds in an aura of objective fact so they can be treated less painfully. The psyche puts an event into another time so it can be treated in another style, such as we would use to treat any historical event, with a certain quality of respect, bemused curiosity, and dispassionate inquiry—and above all by gathering its cultural context. Historicizing is less a sign of psychological defensiveness than of the psyche getting out from under the ego's domination.

Historicizing, moreover, puts events into another genre. Neither here and now, nor once upon a time, but halfway between. Yet this *between* has a precise locus in history and an event placed there may require treatment in the style of that historical time.

Not all psychological complexes appearing as dream figures and symptoms are up to date, asking for a today kind of therapy. There are parts of me that live in old-fashioned stories, stories told even before I was born. They shrink at Rolfing and Esalen, might even fall into a faint, have an attack of vapors, or dry up in *acedia*, were they forced "to weekend." Some of these parts live still on the frontier in a fundamentalist stockade, or at Versailles before the revolution, or betray attitudes of nineteenth-century colonialism or the stealthy upholstered eroticism of Freud's Vienna. The historical fictions that the psyche uses to tell us where we are also tell the kind of therapy called for. Full-blown hysteria in the classical sense of Charcot, Janet, and Freud exists best in that historical context, and should it appear in a contemporary patient that historical context is likewise reappearing complete with its suffocating stage-set. Symptoms are a way of entering history: other times, other complaints. History is a way of entering symptoms.

There is still more to historicizing. Why is history mainly about kings and decisive battles and declarations, about great inventions, ages, and empires? The past is presented as a monument, things that have gone down in history, so that we assume only what matters is historicized, is given the dignity of history.

History enhances, dignifies. When Renaissance writers turned to the past,[39] it was part of their concern for dignity; the past was a means of dignifying the present. We historicize to give the events of our lives a dignity that they cannot receive from contemporaneousness. Here historicizing moves events halfway back toward the once-upon-a-time, toward the sacred and eternal. Any petty event of merely personal life, Napoleon's breakfasts, Luther's farts, when historicized, immediately takes on another significance, echoes with metaphor, moves from description to symbol. History dignifies because it moves events onto the stage of history, becoming thereby tragic, epic, and imaginative. Historians, however, often lose the imaginative function of their work. For them history is a giant supersonic complexity constructed in a darkened hangar by hundreds of workmen organizing millions of parts. But once wheeled on the tarmac it is an image, and was an image all along. The nuts and bolts disappear into a silver vision.

It is this approach to the case history that revitalizes it. My story is a grey complexity of nuts and bolts, all the metallic tediousness of what went wrong and who was right, and yet in that case history is my image, my dignity, my monument. And in it is history itself: my mother had a mother and behind her an ethnic ancestral stream; the son with whom I battle is today, and tomorrow too. There is no part of my personal record that is not at the same time the record of a community, a society, a nation, an age.

The implication is: if history dignifies, then case history as a form of historical writing does so too. In our case history is our human dignity even if that history be written by Zola, Genet, Spillane, or Dickens. Even if it is a tale of degradation and written with sentimentality, even if presented as a wholly literal rope of facts to hang one up in a clinical diagnosis, a case history, because it is history and therefore fiction, is a move into imagination.

For it is the imagination that gives distance and dignity, allowing us to see *events as images*. It is the imagination that stands halfway between the world of now and the imperceptible eternalities of the spirit. Back of history is Mnemosyne (Memoria), the imaginal, mother of historicizing, the soul's archetypal, *sui generis* process of musing in terms of history.

History is a way of musing upon oneself, and case history which too is an expression of Clio, is one of the ways the therapeutic profession and the patients can muse therapeutically. That it does not succeed, that it creates degradation and diagnosis rather than detachment and dignity only points again to the power of story in determining who we are. But the possibility for revisioning and enhancing who we are lies within the events of each case history, if we learn to read it as a fiction and its events as images of Memoria, and she needs remembering in order to create.

10. *The Gift of Case History*

I have found that the person with a sense of story built in from childhood is in better shape than one who has not had stories, who has not heard them, read them, acted them, or made them up. And here I mean oral story, those depending mainly on speech—and reading too has an oral aspect even when one reads alone in silence—rather than story watched on screen or in a picture book. (The preference for word over eye I will explain in a moment.) Story coming on early puts a person into familiarity with the validity of story. One knows what stories can do, how they can make up worlds and transpose existence into these worlds. One maintains a sense of the imaginal world, its convincingly real existence, that it is peopled, that it can be entered and left, that it is always there with its fields and palaces, its dungeons and long ships waiting. One learns that worlds are made by words and not only by hammers and wires.

Screened, watched stories are different because they enter imagination via perception, reinforcing the confusion between perceptual pictures and imaginative images. Pictures we perceive with our sense perceptions; images we imagine. Or, as Edward Casey[40] puts it: an image is not a content that we see but a way in which we see. We may see pictures as images, and a filmed picture may be imagined and become an image; but these images usually remained linked with the visualities in which they first appeared. Word-images, however, are immediate property of imagination, which in turn may visualize them in a mock-perceptual way (like visualizing scenes to music, or faces for fictional characters, or locations in novels); but the essence of word-images is that they are free from the perceptible world and free one from it. They take the mind home, to its poetic base, to the imaginal.

Again it was Freud who rediscovered the difference between perceptual and imaginative images. Actual pictures—Mom and Pop in bed on Saturday afternoon—did not have the recollecting power, the symptom-making force, of the story and images of The Primal Scene. To paraphrase Casey: a trauma is not what happened but the way we see what happened. A trauma is not a pathological event but a pathologized image, an image that has become "intolerable" as Lopez-Pedraza puts it.

If we are ill because of these intolerable images, we get well because of imagination. Poesis as therapy.

The person having had his stories early has had his imagination exercised as an activity. He can *imagine life*, and not only think, feel, perceive, or learn it. And he recognizes that imagination is a place where one can be, a kind of being. Moreover, he has met pathologized images, fantasy figures that are maimed, foolish, sexually obscene, violent and cruel, omnipotently beautiful and seductive. Therapy is one way to revivify the imagination and exercise it. The entire therapeutic business is this sort of imaginative exercise. It picks up again the oral tradition of telling stories; therapy re-stories life. Of course we have to go back to childhood to do this, for that is where our society and we each have placed imagination. [41] Therapy has to be so concerned with the childish part of us in order to recreate and exercise the imagination.

They who still hold to the rationalist and associationist theory of mind and the positivist theory of man will argue that there can be too much fantasy, that it is a flight from reality, and that the task of therapy is precisely the reverse of what I have sketched. Therapy, they hold, is the gradual trimming of imagination and bringing it into service of realistic goals. What makes a man or woman insane, they say, is precisely being overwhelmed with fantasy. Too much story, story confused with history, realities gone.

But the imaginative schools of therapy, sensitively discussed by Mary Watkins in her pioneering book *Waking Dreams*, move straight into fantasy. They take quite literally that therapists are workers in story. Unfortunately this can lead them to dispense with case history as only outer, forgetting that this history too is a piece of imagination, and all the figures in it, including those ever-present traumatic figures, Mom and Pop, are not pictures in memory but images of memoria, with archetypal echo, progenitors in my genealogy myth, who continue to engender my soul by the fantasies and emotions they continue to cause. Case history is not the place of hang-ups to be left behind; it too is a waking dream giving as many marvels as any descent into the cavern of the dragon or walk through the paradise gardens. One need but read each literal sentence of one's life metaphorically, see each picture of the past as an image.

Finally, we recognize that the case history in psychology is a genuine psychic event, an authentic expression of the soul, a fiction created not by the doctor but by the historicizing activity of the psyche, and that this genre of telling corresponds with the reemergence of soul in our age through depth analysis. As depth psychology invented a new kind of practitioner and patient, a new language, a new style of ritual, and of loving, so it shaped a new genre of story, one that is neither biographical nor medical, nor confessional witness, but a narrative of the inner workings of the soul through time, a history of memories, dreams, reflections, sometimes disguised, but not necessarily, in empirical realities. No matter who writes them, they remain documents of the soul.

The lonely analyst in his lamplit *Schreibstube*, the social worker chain-smoking, typing under pressure—the very urge to write these tales, though they go unpublished and unread, is a psychological gesture, itself a telling. For this new form of fiction enters our age driven with fierce compulsion. We want to get it down; there is so much to tell about. This craven trivia is so momentously important because history is now taking place in the soul and the soul has again entered history. Therapists are the new historians. [42]

It is in this sense that case histories are fundamental to depth psychology. Not as empirical fundamentals or residues of the medical model, nor as paradigmatic examples demonstrating one or another theorist's plot do they earn our attention. They are subjective phenomena, soul stories. Their chief importance is for the character about whom they are written, you and me. They give us a narrative, a literary fiction that deliteralizes our life from its projective obsession with outwardness by putting it into a story. They move us from the fiction of reality to the reality of fiction.

They present us with the chance to recognize ourselves in the mess of the world as having been engaged and always being engaged in soul-making, [43] where 'making' returns to its original meaning of *poiesis*. Soul-making as psychological *poiesis*, the making of soul through the imagination of words. [44]

Perhaps our age has gone to analysis not to be loved or get cured, or even to Know Thyself. Perhaps we go to be given a case history, to be told into a soul story and given a plot to live by. This is the gift of case history, the gift of finding oneself in myth. In myths Gods and humans meet.

2

The Pandaemonium of Images

The Pandaemonium of Images
Jung's Contribution to Know Thyself[1]

"It is not possible to speak rightly about the Gods without the Gods." —*Iamblichus*

1. Jung's Daimones

When we inquire into Jung's contribution to our culture, one virtue appears to me to stand out. Jung gave a distinct response to our culture's most persistent psychological need—from Oedipus to Socrates through Hamlet and Faust—Know Thyself. Not only did Jung take this maxim as the leitmotif of his own life, but he gave us a method by which we may each respond to this fundamental question of self-knowledge. It is to this *how*, the art or method of proceeding with oneself, which is as well the grounding impetus within all psychology, that we can especially learn from Jung. So, the angle I wish to develop here is Jung's psychological method as his most valuable gift to us.

You may remember how this began: it is told by Aniela Jaffe in Jung's autobiography. Jung was deluged by "an incessant stream of fantasies," a "multitude of psychic contents and images." In order to cope with the storms of emotion, he wrote down his fantasies and let the storms transpose themselves into images.

You remember also when this took place: it happened shortly after the break with Freud—so much so that Stanley Leavy[2] has suggested that the Salome in the vision which I shall soon come to is none other than a disguised Lou Andreas-Salomé, and the Elijah none other than Freud. At this moment in his life Jung was spiritually alone. But in this isolation he turned neither to a new group, nor to organized religion, nor to refuge in psychosis, nor to security in conventional activities, work, or family: he turned to his images. When there was nothing else to hold to, Jung turned

53

to the personified images of interior vision. He entered into an interior drama, took himself into an imaginative fiction and then, perhaps, began his healing—even if it has been called his breakdown. There, he found a place to go that was no longer Vienna, figures to communicate with who were no longer the psychoanalytic circle of colleagues, and a counsellor who was no longer Freud. This encounter with these personal figures became the first personifications of his mature *fate*—which is also how Jung speaks of the personifications we meet when we interiorize to Know Thyself.[3] It was in this time, during which the dove-maiden spoke to him in a crucial dream, that Jung found his vocation, his psychological faith, and a sense of personality.[4] It is from this point onward that Jung becomes that extraordinary pioneering advocate of the reality of the psyche.

We have looked at *how* and *when;* now the *what* and *who.* What was the content of the first visions and whom did Jung meet? The autobiography says:

> In order to seize hold of the fantasies, I frequently imagined a steep descent. I even made several attempts to get to the very bottom. . . . It was like a voyage to the moon, or a descent into empty space. . . . I had the feeling that I was in the land of the dead. . . the other world. . . . I caught sight of two figures, an old man with a white beard and a beautiful young girl. I summoned up my courage and approached them as though they were real people, and listened attentively to what they told me.[5]

I cite this passage in detail because it is the key to the method; we can take it as an instructor's manual.

The figures whom Jung encountered were Elijah, Salome, and a black serpent. Soon Elijah transformed into Philemon, of whom Jung says:

> Philemon was a pagan and brought with him an Egypto-Hellenistic atmosphere with a Gnostic coloration. . . . Philemon and other figures of my fantasies brought home to me the crucial insight that there are things in the psyche which I do not produce, but which produce themselves and have their own life.[6]

The cosmos brought by Elijah, Salome, the black serpent, and Philemon— this "Egypto-Hellenistic atmosphere with a Gnostic coloration"—was the very one that could sustain the act which Jung was performing. I can hardly stress this enough: the figures whom Jung first met and who convinced him of the reality of their psychic being by extending to him personal relations with the powers of the psyche, these figures derive from the Hellenistic world and its belief in daimons. (*Daimon* is the original Greek spelling for these figures who later became *demons* because of the Christian view and *daemons* in positive contradistinction to that view.)

Jung's descent to the "land of the dead" presented him with his spiritual ancestors, who, through Jung, ushered in a new daimonology and angelogy.

Know Thyself in Jung's manner means to become familiar with, to open oneself to and listen to, that is, to know and discern, daimons. Entering one's interior story takes a courage similar to starting a novel. We have to engage with persons whose autonomy may radically alter, even dominate, our thoughts and feelings, neither ordering these persons about nor yielding to them full sway. Fictional and factual, they and we, are drawn together like threads into a *mythos*, a plot, until death do us part. It is a rare courage that submits to this middle region of psychic reality where the supposed surety of fact and illusion of fiction exchange their clothes.

Just to remind us what a radical, shattering move—theological, epistemological, ontological—Jung's personifying was, let me merely pronounce the usual judgement upon daimons that is part of our Western religious psychology. Whether Eastern Church or Roman, whether Old Testament or New, whether Protestant or Catholic—daimons are no good things. They are part of the world of Satan, of Chaos, of Temptation. They have been written against by major Christian theologians down through the centuries, associated with the cult of serpent worship in the midst of Christian Europe, and they are, according to the authority of Matthew's Gospel,[7] the source of possession, sickness, and magic.

Who indeed are these figures that they should be so menacing? If we look into the world before and parallel with the rise of Christianity—first to Homer, then to Plato and the dramatists, then to Plutarch, Plotinus, Iamblichus, and then to the Renaissance—the *daimones*[8] were figures of the middle realm, neither quite transcendent Gods nor quite physical humans, and there were many sorts of them, beneficial, terrifying, message-bringers, mediators, voices of guidance and caution (as Socrates' Daimon and as Diotima). Even Eros was a *daimon.*

But the dogmatic crystallization of our religious culture demonized the daimons. As a fundamental component of polytheistic paganism, they had to be negated and denied by Christian theology which projected its repression upon the daimons, calling *them* the forces of denial and negation. Thus Jung's move which turned directly to the images and figures of the middle realm was a heretical, demonic move. His move into the imagination, which had been forced upon him by his fantasies and emotions, had already been prejudged in our religious language as demonic and in our clinical language as multiple personality or as schizophrenia. Yet, this radical activation of imagination was Jung's method of Know Thyself.

His move between the two orthodoxies of theological religion and clinical scientism re-established in experience the middle realm which he was to call 'psychic reality.' This psychic reality discovered by Jung consists in fictive figures. It is poetic, dramatic, literary in nature. The Platonic *metaxy* speaks in mythical fictions. Freud's fictioning appeared disguised in his case histories and his cosmogonic theories; Jung's appeared overtly in the history of his own case. Freud entered the literary imagination by writing about other people; Jung by envisioning himself as 'other people.' What we learn from Freud is that this literary imagination goes on in the midst of historical fact. What we learn from Jung is that this literary imagination goes on in the midst of ourselves. Poetic, dramatic fictions are what actually people our psychic life. Our life in soul is a life in imagination.

We have already been given the clue in the instructor's manual as to how this third realm traditionally called 'soul' can be re-established—and by anyone. Jung says he treated the figures whom he met "as though they were real people." The key is that *as though*; the metaphorical, as-if reality, neither literally real (hallucinations or people in the street) nor irreal/unreal ('mere' fictions, projections which 'I' make up as parts of 'me', auto-suggestive illusions). In an 'as-if' consciousness they are powers with voice, body, motion, and mind, fully felt but wholly imaginary. This is psychic reality, and it comes in the shape of daimons. By means of these daimonic realities, Jung confirmed the autonomy of the soul. His own experience connected again the realm of daimons with that of soul. And ever since his move, soul and daimons imply, even require, each other.

2. Introspection

Briefly, let us look at the question of introspection in order to recognize just why Jung's approach to Know Thyself is radical, not only philosophically and theologically, but also to see it as a new, important step in psychology.

When you or I attempt to know ourselves, what are the ways we might proceed? We can ask others. We can take tests: projective ones of our inner fantasies (Rorschach); inventory ones of our psychological contents; comparative ones, like intelligence tests, that rate our faculties and skills in relation with standards drawn from other persons. We can remember; we can associate backward and downward into the forgotten and repressed. We can look at our deeds, and to what we have made of what we have been through—biography. [9] We can free our 'true selves' from our daily selves by altering our state of consciousness, whether in the manners suggested by Plato in his four kinds of *mania*, or in modern methods of release therapies. We can love: for, as some hold, only in loving is our self made visible and knowable. (This last implies that you cannot fully or ever Know Thyself, but only reveal thyself; we can be known, but not know.)

This diversity of answers betrays a premise of archetypal psychology, that is, there are a multiplicity of answers to all major, archetypal, sorts of questions, depending upon the God and the mytheme which informs our answer, whether detached and Apollonic, abstracted and Saturnian, a God of Love or Dionysian release, of Heroic deeds or Hephaestian artifacts. There seems no single way of knowing thyself, even if psychology has favored the method of introspection.

Introspection is intimately tied with the history of psychology. Perhaps modern psychology arose out of the introspective tendency and is an objectification and systematization of the attempt at a detached observation of consciousness. We can find roots of introspection already in Plato: in the *Meno*, for instance, and of course in the behavior of Socrates. We find introspection as the method in Augustine's *Confessions*. And we find introspection to be at the base of modern philosophical psychology from Descartes' *inspectio*, to Locke and Hume, and to Husserl. Here I am leaving quite to one side religious introspection in spiritual disciplines, pietism, examination of conscience, and the like.

Modern introspection as a method begins with Karl Philipp Moritz (1756-93) who moved the pietistic method of self-observation into an Enlightened science. The method culminates in the work of Oswald Kulpe and the Würzburg School. To know thyself, to know the soul, one observes its associations, the way it wills and it remembers, its manners of perceiving, sensing, tasting, feeling, and especially the ways of its cogitation, its pure, imageless thinking modes.

Now the great bankruptcy of this method—and it was bankrupt else it would not have yielded sway so easily to behaviourism on the one hand and to psychoanalysis on the other—is that introspection remains closed into the rational soul. It is ultimately solipsistic. We never get out of our private feelings, thinkings, willings, rememberings. It remains primarily an investigation of the tonalities of ego-consciousness. And where it re-appears today, whether in Merleau-Ponty, in Eugene Gendlin,[10] or in Roger Poole,[11] introspection remains an *inspectio* of the Cartesian ego. Or, in the mythological terms of an archetypal psychology, this method is an ego enactment of Apollo-Helios.

So what of the depths? Can we inspect them from above and in sunlight? So, it cannot help but be a sunlit detaching observation even when it tries most to focus upon gut-feelings. Hence the feelings that emerge appear in conceptual language, words like anxiety, guilt, hopelessness, hostility—abstractions shorn of imagery. The actual idiopathic body is smoothed and formulated into nomothetic words representing that body. This subtle substitution of actual feelings by conceptualized feelings dried-out in Apollonian sunlight results from the Cartesian process of introspection. Or must we not, like Jung, descend into them? When you or I struggle with a crucial confusion, is it possible to introspect to the root of the problem? Can one introspect the bottom of despair or the source of anxiety? Turning inward, we draw a blank.

Writers know they cannot introspect their characters. Their scenes come of themselves and their figures speak, walk in and out. With few people is a writer more intimate than with his characters and yet they continue to surprise him with their autonomy. Besides, they are not concerned with 'me' but with the world they inhabit and which refers to me, the introspector, only obliquely. The act of turning to imagination is not an act of introspection: it is a negative capability, a willful suspension of disbelief in them and of belief in oneself as their author. The relativization of the author—who is making up whom, who is writing whom—goes along with the fictional mode—in the course of active imagination one wavers between losing control and putting words in their mouths. But introspection will not solve even this problem, only the act of fictioning further. Introspection simply returns one to the literalism of subjectivity. We have taken the notion of subjectivity so literally that we now believe in an imaginary subject at the beginning of each sentence who does the work, a subject pre-fixing each verb. But the work is done by the verbs themselves; they are fictioning, actively imagining, not I. The action is in the plot, inaccessible to introspection, and only the characters know what's going on. As Philemon taught Jung: you are not the author of the play of the psyche.

Moreover, and more important than the act itself, *who* is doing the introspection? Is it not the same old 'I'? How can we introspect this introspector? How can we relativize the observer and move deeper than the subject who is trying to know so as to discover a psychic objectivity that is not determined by the I?

For psychic objectivity, or what Jung calls the objective psyche, we require first of all psychic objects, powers that relentlessly obstruct the ego's path as obstacles, obsessions, obtrusions. And this is precisely how Jung speaks of the complexes as Gods or daimons that cross our subjective will. [12]

Complexes do not respond to worry, to searching parties, to naturalists with tags and labels. The "little people" (as Jung called the complexes) scurry into the bush the moment one's attention is turned toward them. Likewise, they cannot be found by just letting-go, as if they would come up the moment we lie down. Relaxed, body-referent introspection is conceived still in the language of will. (Besides, an image or body-sensation that is an illustration of what we are already experiencing in consciousness is merely an allegory; it is merely the same known content depicted in another medium.) The complexes in the deep have their own body and their own will, and this is not bound to the ego's by laws of compensation. Therefore, humanistic therapies never get below the human in man, nor can they leave his subjectivity. The entire existentialist procedure of man's choosing by making up his mind after searching himself or sinking into himself, is based on an introspection that omits the little people. Their points of view are given often only when *not* asked for, as the visitations or interferences beyond ego-consciousness. Can we summon angels? Do they obey the principle of compensation?

Perhaps this is why Nietzsche, Dilthey, and Jung are each severely sceptical of the value of usual introspection. Dilthey [13] insisted that introspection would never suffice to grasp human nature, but that history would. Nietzsche wrote: "Immediate self-observation is not enough, by a long way, to enable us to learn how to know ourselves. We need history, for the past continues to flow through us in a hundred channels." [14] If we translate Nietzsche's and Dilthey's 'history' into 'collective unconscious,' we approximate the position of Jung in regard to Know Thyself.

Know Thyself, here, means to know the unconsciousness of history, and particularly how it is at work in the 'I', the 'objective' introspector itself. As long as this 'I' is the historical ego, unconsciously reflecting the history which formed it and which its continuity would uphold, all that we discover in our introspections will be shaped in our own historical image. I will be forced to believe that the figures whom I encounter are parts of 'me,' projections of 'me.' I will rightly assess them as mere phantoms, shadows which I have cast, and I will disdain them.

But thereby I will miss that opening step into Know Thyself which these images of myself-in-them afford—for they are, first of all, my shadows depicting my historical situation. They offer the opportunity of recognizing history's hundred channels (like Jung's Siegfried and his Biblical images) that are actually determining my consciousness.

Of prime importance here is recognizing that these little people do come from the land of the dead. Like Jung's Philemon and Salome, they are legendary personages of history, showing culture at work in the channels of the soul. The land of the dead is the country of ancestors, and the images who walk in on us are our ancestors. If not literally the blood and genes from whom we descend, then they are the historical progenitors, or archetypes, of our particular spirit informing it with ancestral culture.

After this historical recognition—the image as ancestor—there is the experience of the *claim* that images make upon me. This is the moral moment in imagination. Imaginational morality is essentially *not* in my judgement as to whether the daimons I behold are good or bad, *nor* does it lie in the application of imagination (how I put what I discover from images into life's actions). Rather this morality lies in recognizing the images religiously, as powers with claims. Jung puts this ethical question in the same chapter we have been quoting. He says:

> I took great care to try to understand every single image . . . and, above all, to realize them in actual life. That is what we usually neglect to do. We allow images to rise up, and maybe we wonder about them, but that is all. We do not take the trouble to . . . draw ethical conclusions. . . It is equally a grave mistake to think that it is enough to gain some understanding of the images. . . . Insight into them must be converted into an ethical obligation. . . . The images . . . place a great responsibility upon a man. [15]

Here Jung attributes the moral moment to the responding ego, whereas I would psychologize the question further, asking why does the moral question arise at all in his mind after the encounter with images? Possibly the moral concern is the result of the encounter itself and so enters Jung's narrative at this juncture. [16] As these imaginal figures bring a sense of internal fate, so they bring an awareness of internal necessity and its limitations. We feel responsible to them and for them. A mutual caring envelopes the relationship, or, as this situation was put in antiquity, the daimones are also guardian spirits. Our images are our keepers, as we are theirs.

From the outside, the appearance of the daimons seems to offer ethical relativity: a paradise of seductions and escapades. But this fantasy of ethical relativity betrays a consciousness that is not yet inside the imaginal world, that does not Know Thyself from within its images. In other words, the question of ethical relativity which raises its head whenever one speaks of a "pandaemonium of images" and a plurality of Gods is answered by the dedication which the images demand. It is they—not we—who demand meticulous crafting into jewelled idols; they, who call for ritualized devotions, who insist they be consulted before we act. Images are the compelling source of morality and religion as well as the conscientiousness of art. And, as we do not make them up, so we do not make up our response to them, but are 'taught' this response by them as moral instances. It is when we lose the images that we become moralistic, as if the morality contained within the images becomes a dissociated, free-floating guilt, a conscience without face.

When an image is realized—fully imagined as a living being other than myself—then it becomes a *psychopompos*, a guide with a soul having its own inherent limitation and necessity. It is this image and no other, so that the conceptual questions of moral pluralism and relativism fade in front of the actual engagement with the image. The supposed creative pandaemonium of the teeming imagination is limited to its phenomenal appearance in a particular image, that specific one which has come to me pregnant with significance and intention, a necessary angel as it appears here and now and which teaches the hand to represent it, the ear to hear, and the heart how to respond. There is thus revealed through this engagement a *morality of the image*. Psychological morality which derives from the imaginal is no longer a 'new ethics' of shadow integration by means of that same old Kantian ego and its heroic wrestlings with abstract dualisms. The ego is no longer the place where morality resides, a philosophical position that had wrested morality from the imagination thereby demonizing it. Instead, it is the daimon who is our preceptor, our *spiritus rector*.

Here Carl Gustav Jung and Elijah-Philemon reenter. As the autobiography puts it:

> In my fantasies I held conversations with him [Philemon], and he said things which I had not consciously thought.... He said I treated thoughts as if I generated them myself, but in his view thoughts were like animals in the forest, or people in a room, or birds in the air.... It was he who taught me psychic objectivity, the reality of the psyche. [17]

This method of active imagination which Jung inaugurated in modern psychology is an answer to the classical question of introspection at such a profound level that it changes the image of human being, of the psyche, and what Know Thyself essentially means. Before Freud, knowing thyself in psychology meant to know one's ego-consciousness and its functions. Then with Freud Know Thyself extended to mean knowing one's past personal life, a whole life recalled. But after Jung, Know Thyself means an archetypal knowing, a daimonic knowing. It means a familiarity with a host of psychic figures from geographical, historical, and cultural contexts, a

hundred channels beyond my personal identity. After Jung, I cannot pretend to know myself unless I know the archetypes—"The conception of
them as *daimonia* is therefore quite in accord with their nature," says Jung. [18]
And I meet these peculiar creatures both as images in the imagination and
as the archetypal patterns moving within my consciousness.

3. *Jaspers' Attack on Demonology*

We turn now to Karl Jaspers for a critical attack upon demonology. Let
us give this opponent the floor, because in this difference between Jaspers
and Jung is the grand difference between spirit and soul, [19] between philosophy and psychology, between monism and polycentricity, between
abstraction and personification, between the literal and the literary,
between existential humanism and archetypal psychologizing, between
ego and anima. In listening now to Jaspers I ask you to keep in mind Jung's
method of speaking with his inner persons, and our individual experiences
of active imagination, our inner journeys, our dreams. Jaspers writes:

> We call demonology a conception which makes being reside in
> powers, in effective form-constituting forces, constructive and
> destructive, that is in demons, benevolent and malignant, in many
> gods; these powers are perceived as directly evident, and the percep-
> tions are translated as a doctrine. Good and evil alike are hallowed,
> and the whole is enhanced by gazing into dark depths that are man-
> ifested in images...; it passes as an immanent transcendence... and
> ... is necessarily split into many forces. [20]

Jaspers finds demonology appropriate to myth and to the classical world.
But when the transcendent God appeared as an alternative, then "demonology vanished or was brought under control" (p. 119). Thus to revive "this
mythological mode of thought" in our present world is an illusion, for
"there are no demons" (*idem*). He reports on Goethe and then Kierkegaard,
summing up his critique in these six points (pp. 125-28): Modern
demonology (1) "misses transcendence" because "the gods have become
world," (2) "the individual man has no irreplaceable value;" (3) "no relation
to the one is gained... fragmentation...; man splits into his potentialities

. . . ;everything can be justified;" (4) "Demonology is submerged in nature
. . . ; man loses his distinction from nature;" (5) "Modern demonology is
purely an aesthetic attitude. . . . Man no longer need commit himself,
because for every situation he has a stock of aesthetic images with their
illusory grandeur;" last—and crucial—(6) "demonology sets up an intermediary form of being that is neither empirical reality nor transcendent
actuality. . . . ;everything that is not either world (as demonstrable reality)
or God is deception and illusion. . . . There is God and the world and
nothing in between."

I have let Jaspers lead the charge against the daimons, but I could have
called also upon Karl Barth who describes the daimons as powers of chaos
and forces of negativity that lie and deny; since the "triumph of Jesus Christ
over the daemons, they have no more to say (nichts zu melden)"[21] Or,
Teilhard de Chardin: ". . . the One joined in battle with. . . this non-
existent multiplicity which stood in opposition to the One by way of
defiant contradiction. To create is to condense, to concentrate, to
organize, to unify."[22]

For Jaspers, Barth, and Teilhard, the daimons are a pandaemonium: by
nature they are multiple (like the sparks of consciousness in our complexes).[23] And though they are "non-existent" and "have nothing to say,"
they contradict and require battle. This battle is against the force of multiplicity. Human internal diversity which makes possible our internal
conflicts and self-differentiation, the complexities of Know Thyself—or
individuation in Jung's view—is in their view daemonic.

By imagining the daimons as contradiction, a question arises concerning
their ability to speak. This question was already in classical and Christian[24]
minds; and if they could speak, then in what language? Plotinus (Enneads,
IV 3, 18) considered that the daimons and souls might well use speech. But
one of the ways of depotentiating polytheism by Christian writers was to
deny the power of the word (the Logos) to inner voices. The only true
Logos was Christ. To open the door to inner voices lets in the powers of
darkness, the daimons of antique religion, polytheism, and heresy.[25]

So you see that an introspection, which follows the path of imagination
by listening to and speaking with inner images, means meeting with
daimons. Psychology of the depths is therefore forced ultimately to tangle
with that huge theological bugbear—demonology—as Jaspers keenly recognized.

The denial of daimons and their exorcism has been part and parcel of Christian psychology, leaving the Western psyche few means but the hallucinations of insanity for recognizing daimonic reality. By refusing even the possibility of more than one voice—except the voice of the devil—all *daimones* became demonic and anti-Christian in their message, and in their very multiplicity. Of course classical introspection stopped short and could not get out of the ego. Introspection's course and limits were set by a consciousness that insisted on unity. To hear the deeps not only affronted Christian tradition; it invited what had been declared the Devil, Hell, and madness. (Again, Jung's case is witness.)

Today we call the internal policing of the psyche by an *inspectio* become inspector general 'mind control.' Here we begin to see the staggering consequences of denial of the daimons: it leaves the psyche bereft of all persons but the ego, the controller who becomes super-ego. No spontaneous fantasy, image, or feeling may be independent of this unified ego. Every psychic happening becomes 'mine.' Know Thy*self* shifts to Know *My*self. What Philemon taught Jung, however, was that there are things in the psyche that are no more "mine" than "animals in the forest . . . or birds in the air." Moreover, without images, the imaginative perspective itself withers, only reinforcing the ego's literalism. It is therefore of little wonder that the Christian tradition continued to blame this same ego which it had fostered for its sin of pride and chastised it with humility. The images which could teach the ego its limits, as Philemon taught Jung, having been repressed, only return unimaged as archetypal delusions in the midst of subjective consciousness itself. The ego becomes demonic. It fully believes in its own power.

Returning to Jaspers' six critiques, let us try—not to refute them—but to see through them. Let us try to ascertain which archetypal factor he is attacking because this archetype might be intolerable to the perspective that is dominating his viewpoint. By revealing this background, we can understand his points in quite a different light, even re-valuing them in support of Jung.

First: The demonology of active imagination "misses transcendence" because to Know Thyself—the aim of psychology of all schools—is to know immanence, the worlds within and below visible behavior. The Gods are in the world, not beyond the world. Transcendence is spirit language; immanence is psychological, or soul, language. [26]

Second: "The individual man has no irreplaceable value" because Jung's psychology is less concerned with personality as individualism than with individuation as an *impersonal* psychic process which is the ultimate giver of value. Value arises not from man as in humanism, but from what is behind and within man, soul, *anima*. Psychology is soul-centered, not man-centered as is existential humanism.

Third: "No relation to the one is gained." Of course Jung spent much energy on the "relation to the one." But Jung did not force this, did not foresake plurality and multiplicity for the sake of an arbitrary and abstract unity. [27] Wholeness and completion are not only unity; they are a concatenation of quite specific oppositions. Individuation, according to Jung, is a process of differentiating, of differing, of recognizing the many complexes, voices, and persons that we each are.

Fourth: "Demonology is submerged in nature." Yes, says Jung, this is precisely what active imagination intends to do: submerge modern man again into nature for this is what he has lost—the archaic, instinctual response. And this response of nature appears as the archetypal image, because archetypes are also instincts. Where Jaspers divides transcendence and nature, Jung keeps instinctual nature as the very place of the transcendent archetypes. "The old wise man is really an ape," said Jung.

Fifth: "Modern demonology is a purely aesthetic attitude." Again Jung agrees in condemning the aesthetic attitude, especially when confronting images. [28] But Jung takes it further by asking a psychological question of this "attitude," discovering that it conceals the charming smiles and wiles and guiles of the anima. This means that aestheticism belongs to soul. If we follow Jaspers, this aesthetic attitude becomes demonic; if we follow Jung, we may recognize the person within aestheticism, keeping it within the psychological opus by giving it value and something to do (painting, writing, forming) in realizing the imagination. Clearly, the second, fourth and fifth critiques point to the anima.

Sixth: Demonology sets up an intermediate form of being neither empirical nor transcendent; this, as well as Jaspers' either/or disjunction ("there is God and the world and nothing in between"), must be looked at more attentively.

Jaspers is holding to the two-worlds system: [29] spirit and matter, philosophy and science, God and Nature, sacred and secular, mind and body—

however you wish to speak of it. The intermediate alternative which he cannot allow is the third realm of the Platonic tradition to which Jung also holds and in which his entire thought and life is based. *"Esse in anima,"* Jung calls it; to be in soul, an ontology of soul. This third realm both mediates between the two worlds of Jaspers and maintains distinctions between them.[30] Jaspers, here, recognizes that the commitment to daimons affirms psychic reality, an as-if mode that is both like and different from empirical and metaphysical perspectives and that offers a way of relating both in terms of soul.

In other words, Jaspers has been making our point for us, although in reverse. By taking the transcendent position of Protestant monotheism—with nothing in between God and the world—he is obliged to deny the psychic reality of the daimons. He stays always within the archetypal perspective of philosophy with its commitment to coherent unity. His ennobled notion of man affirms, and inflates, the ego reflecting this transcendent unity, an ego which must see multiplication only as fragmentation. Jaspers well perceives the dangers in demonology, but not its prospective possibility for releasing the soul from its history of ego-domination. Because Jaspers treats the question metaphysically, in the language of 'is' verbs, (*"are* there demons or not"), for him the issue is one of substance and being. Were it treated psychologically, the daimons would be considered first as experiences, personified perspectives toward events, and demonology as a mode of imagining. But to approach the issue in this fashion, psychologically, requires an appreciation of the image, and anima.

Anima is the true target of his attack. His critique of demonology is more basically an attack on psychic reality, *esse in anima*, the anima factor that aestheticizes, that personifies, who keeps us "submerged in nature" and does not want to lift up to transcendence, who insists soul is as irreplaceable as man, and who refuses the dichotomy of either/or that would obliterate its ambiguous place of being.

This anima factor, banned from his existential thought, then returns in Jaspers' own existence as irritability and petulance when he writes in the same essay (p. 25): "This demonology is as hard to apprehend as Proteus, it is a nothingness that takes on constantly new disguises and in its multiformity makes use of all the old twists of the demonic."

Here our antagonist has been caught by *anima mercurii*, the mercurial soul that Jung too compares to Proteus, [31] who was the most favored 'divinity' during the Renaissance's return to the soul and its images.

I have not quite done with the Jaspers question. It is not easy to leave, for his position condenses the philosophical, theological, and humanist-existential arguments against Jung's accomplishment.

This accomplishment was not a wilful resurrection of myths[32] and daimons, nor an act of heresy, mystical politics, or magic theurgy, as Jaspers' critique implies. Rather, Jung's occupation with daimons came from the necessity of his fate breaking through in a psychopathological crisis. Curiously, psychopathology was a field in which Jaspers made a lasting mark with a profound and brilliant work. Yet he left this field early. I believe we can see also the background to that departure and to Jaspers' hatred of psychoanalysis, of which he once said "the devil has so deeply taken hold of that. . . I believe every physician who follows this path to be in jeopardy."[33] The physician who would stay with the patient's psychopathology must go to the depths where Jaspers would not tread. His metaphysics allowed no third ambiguous place. He could not become, as did Jung, a 'daimonic man.' For psychopathology is a description in functional language of the same phenomena treated by demonology in the language of personified contents.

Jung puts this question of psychopathology as follows:

> Every split off portion of libido, every complex has or is a (fragmentary) personality . . . when we go into the matter more deeply, we find that they are really archetypal formations. There are no conclusive arguments against the hypothesis that these archetypal figures are endowed with personality at the outset and are not just secondary personalizations. In so far as the archetypes do not represent mere functional relationships, they manifest themselves as *daimones*, as personal agencies. [34]

It is these personified agencies of the imagination—what the Art of Memory called *imagines agentes*[35]—that compose the history of each case. The life of these *diamones* is our psychodynamics and psychopathology. (And, as the ambivalence of the term itself implies, demons are also daimons.) These figures are the ways transcendencies become immanent. As figures of psychic reality they guide us in psychic reality so that we do not turn to guides from empirical naturalism or spiritual transcendentalism. Neither behaviorists nor gurus. As guides they keep us to the myths we are enacting, providing us with continual opportunities for seeing where Satan is truly at work—as Kathleen Raine has shown through her study of Blake. Satan works through his minion, the ego of choice (who would divide the ambivalence of demon/daimon), whether this ego be cloaked in the black cloth of moralism, or in the simple blue cloth of Marxism, or the sober tweeds of positivism, behaviorism, and humanism.

Jung returns to daimones in the "Late Thoughts" of his autiobiography. He explains that he preferred the term 'unconscious,' even while "knowing that I might equally well speak of 'God' or 'daimon'... I am aware that 'mana,' 'daimon,' and 'God' are synonyms for the unconscious—that is to say, we know just as much or as little about them as about the latter." He says "unconscious" was "scientific" and "rational," "neutral" and "commonplace," whereas the use of "mythic language" gives "impetus to the imagination." Jung saw the essential difference between rational and mythic appellations as between 'banal[ity]' and 'numinosity.' But must the line be drawn in this manner, be drawn at all? Does this not set up borders requiring opposite terrains and translations between them? Must mythical imagination be so numinous and conceptual science so banal?

For me, both daimon and unconscious are modes of imagining, modes of writing fictions, and both have their healing efficacy as the case may be. Imagination goes on in the commonplace and in everyday 'unimaginative' language, providing we hear into it for its images or look with an imagining eye. A romantic view of Imagination inflates it so we need sober Science to bring ourselves back from the numinous to the commonplace. If, however, we let imagination out from its exotic borders, extending its definition so as to be the permeating unconscious aspect of all things whatsoever, then the 'dispassionate observation' offered by scientific terms such as "unconscious" is not the only mode of objectification of imagination. Mythic imagination provides another mode, as Jung in this same passage describes.

> The great advantage of... 'daimon' and 'God' lies in making possible a much better objectification of the *vis-à-vis*, namely, a *personification* of it. Their emotional quality confers life and effectuality upon them.

Hate and love, fear and reverence, enter the scene of the confronta-
tion and raise it to a drama. What has merely been 'displayed'
becomes 'acted.'

By throwing up persons, images and voices, the daimonic mode objectifies
and claims emotional participation at the same time. Then we are no longer
just an audience in a theatre (as we discussed above in "Dream, Drama,
Dionysos"), Pentheus in a tree, or entering the fiction as neutral commonplace observer. The personifications disclose the facts just so, quite objectively, just as the facts wish to present themselves in their own voices.

4. Imagism and Iconoclasm

Now let us go behind Jung and Jaspers, far behind, to Nicaea in the
Autumn of the year 787 and the last full ecumenical council where some
three hundred Bishops and their representatives of the Eastern and Western
Churches gathered in Byzantine Bythnia. There a careful distinction was
formulated about the nature of images and the correct relation to them.

You recall that Jaspers' attack on demonology contains this statement:
"We call demonology a conception which makes being reside in powers, in
many gods, and these are perceived as directly evident by gazing into dark
depths that are manifested in images."

You recall also that this is precisely what Jung did do: he gazed into dark
depths, descended, found his new being, the new post-Freudian Jung of esse
in anima, and that this was consequent upon his having turned directly to
images.

So, in order to grasp the depth of difference between Jaspers and Jung as
protagonists of two Weltanschauungen, we go back to Nicaea and 787 for
there the Great Iconoclast Controversy came to head.[36] This controversy
recurs through history: the Bible, Mohammed, Cromwell; it recurs in the
Council of Trent. Perhaps it recurs in modern painting. Iconoclasm vs.
Imagism, or idolatry as the iconoclasts call their enemy.

The iconoclast attack upon the image—which epitomizes the attack of
spirit upon soul—takes place not only in the concrete smashing of statues,
burning of altars, and defacing icons. We continue the iconoclast habit and
destroy images in religion and literature through allegory and in psychol-

ogy through conceptual interpretation. (This kitten in your dream is your feeling function; this dog, your sexual desire; this great snake coiled in the corner is your unconscious, or mother, or anxiety.) The image is slain and stuffed with concepts or vanishes into an abstraction.

As a footnote to that Council and to my suggestion that the issue between iconoclasm and imagism is one between spirit and soul, we find that the sides were drawn then partly along the lines of male versus female. It was the military mainly, the Byzantine soldiers, who destroyed the popular effigies in the villages, while the women in the villages destroyed the soldiers. (The "earliest recorded statue of Christ," by the way, was believed to have been erected by the woman with an issue of blood, Matt. IX. 20-22.)[37] The image of Mary was especially the center of contention, and Empress Irene was responsible for convening the Council on behalf of the imagist faction.

When one reads the canons of that Council,[38] one sees the male-female, spirit-soul argument carried into the tiniest detail, such as rigorous separation of monks and nuns (no singing of "satanic" songs at table, no eating together)—Canons 17-22. As well there were moves against what we might call the aesthetic anima: no "showy apparel," no "gay silken" or "colored decoration" on the bordures of priestly dress—Canon 16. The same sober abstract theological reforming spirit—long before our Western Reformation, but in the same name: the war against images, imagination, anima.

Although the history books say that the imagists won at that Council, I believe a closer psychological reading shows the victor to have been iconoclasm. At Nicaea a subtle differentiation was made between *adoration* of images (idolatry) and the *veneration* of images.[39] The eight sessions of statements emphasized the distinction between the image as such with full divine power and the image as signifying or pointing to that power. It concluded that the divine was *not* inherent in the image; images were not repositories of power. Rather they were useful for didactic purposes. They were not presences or presentation, but representation, illustration and allegories to remind the faithful of abstract theological figuration transcendent to the image.[40]

It was stated as well just which figurations could be imaged—the ones we are used to in Christian traditional iconography. What Jung calls "individual symbol-formation"[41] was disallowed.

One line of the imagists' defense ran like this. Christ himself was an Iconographer, whose very nature necessitated putting on the flesh and taking visible shape. This implies that true Christian service must also serve the image. Images are effects of their co-relative causes, and they have effects because of these causes. Co-relation implies simultaneity; cause and effect are both present together at the same moment: the archetype is *in* the image. Thus, "whoever destroys the effect destroys the cause"[42] One cannot smash an image without at the same moment obliterating an archetype—in this instance, the very Christ!

Besides the many subsidary arguments that found focus in the battle over images, looking back we can see that the principal fight was between a literalist theology of spirit and an imaginational pychology. Or, at least, this is one way of putting that battle. The iconoclasts saw an image as consubstantial in all aspects with its archetype. The depicted image of Christ has full identity with the substance of Christ. Not only is this impossible, they argued, since Christ cannot be circumscribed (except in his fleshly human nature), it is furthermore intolerable, since it implies that God is actually and fully present in the icon. As Sheldon-Williams points out, the iconoclasts identified image and prototype by thinking in the category of *substance*. The iconophils, however, conceived the relation in terms of analogy, thinking in the category of *quality*. The image of Christ is in all aspects like the visible, historical Christ, qualitatively similar, though of course not substantially the same as that Christ.

Although the iconoclasts burdened their enemies with literalism, accusing them of primitive pagan idolatry because they honored statues, the true literalism resides where it always does, not in the object of worship, but in the mind of the worshipper. Metaphysical and physical thinking are two peas in a pod: the one abstract, the other concrete, alike in their inability to grasp the analogical, metaphorical mode of the soul.

Thus the iconoclast controversy becomes less a question of the nature of images and more a question of how we connect with them. Here we can return to St. John Damascene (ca. 675-749)[43] who was the first to work out a serious defense of imagism. The image is not to be approached with *latria*, that kind of worship due the supreme invisible power as object of religion (John Damasc. Pt. III). Or, in our language we might say: do not approach the image in the attitude of the spirit; rather, turn to the image with *dulia*, an attitude of service. It is that psychological attentiveness and careful observation appropriate to the icon of saint or angel, holy place, object or book. *Latria* in relation with a statue is idolatry—as the word itself says. But it is not the image that is the idol; it is the *latria* which makes it such.

For psychology, the healing power of image lies not in a literal, magical effect: if your ear hurts, paint it or hang a tin ear-shaped replica on a shrine. This would be *latria*, an idolatry of the morbid part, ear as idol. *Latria* here assumes a one-to-one relation between ear and image, without the connotative implications of ear, an ear deaf to its own metaphors. (In this regard medicine is like magic: it is utterly literal and idolizes the afflicted part.) The act of painting the image or speaking with it in a poem is *dulia*, a service *to the image* (not the ear) even if we be driven to the act by its pain. Image-work is directed to imagination and by imagination so that if healing comes, it comes through the middle realm of psyche, a healing of the imaginal body, a healing of imagination's middle ear. This kind of healing process by means of image-work depends on a fictional sense: one is in attentive service (*dulia*) within an imaginational reality. The primary intention in image work is to get the image right (rather than the ear). Thus the healing, if it comes, is first of all of our fictional sense, giving a fictional sense even to our ailments. Imagination itself must be cared for since it may well be the source of our ailing.

Latria, and thus idolatry, continues still today in other ways in psychology, whenever, for instance, we take our images as magical messages from The Unconscious, as divine revelations of the Self. A psychology of compensation (the dream image as compensatory reply to ego-consciousness) has replaced the theology of prayer (the dream image as divine response to human beseeching). We have forgotten *dulia*—that it is the human job to serve and care for the images. As St. Basil expressed it, "honor rendered to the image passes to the prototype."[44]

This psychological difference between image as presence and image as representation, between symbol and allegory, continues in our psychology today. When we speak in a Kantian manner of archetypal images as 'representations' of the Great Mother, Self, or Anima, and proceed to treat archetypes as unknowable transcendent realities in themselves beyond the images in which they inhere, move, and have their being, then we have taken the Nicaean position. We have separated archetype and image, noumenon and phenomenon. This move returns us not only to Kant and Protestant iconoclasm, but to the spiritual preference for abstraction— Truth, Beauty, God—as more important, more universal, more eternal than concrete psychological imagination. It is a return to Nicaea and 787.

Jaspers' connection of demonology with images is a recurrence of iconoclasm. Jung's experiential turn to images is the recurrence of the imagist gesture. For it does not matter whether the images are 'out there' as cult statues, that move or wink or nod—(the origin of the word *numinous*, *numen*, refers to the animation of an image, quite a different experience from Rudolf Otto's abstract feeling of a transcendent unimaged Wholly Other)[45]—or whether the images are of the interior imagination, as in Jung's case, the self-moving figures of an animated fantasia. (Philemon-Elijah was accompanied by a beautiful young woman.) What does matter to the iconophil is that which Jaspers condemns: being and power and reality are invested in images. They are numinous because they are animated, soul-charged, whether shaped into external icons or imagined and spoken with in soul.

We have taken Jung's case as a presentation of a method, a handbook telling 'how.' We are further taking Jung's case as *récit* in the sense of Henry Corbin, that is, as a recital of an adventure in or with the imaginal. Adventures such as these open new territories of soul, give soul new ground—or restore to it old ground. Thus, by means of Jung's example and method we are today each able to undo the grip of ancient ecclesiastical fingers upon our imagining hearts. We can each restore the primacy of the image in our individual lives, thereby realizing again the direct relation between image and psyche.

In fact, when Jung formulates his experience, he writes: "Image *is* psyche."[46] So, when I ask, "Where is my soul; how do I meet it; what does it want now?" The answer is: "Turn to your images." Jung writes: "Every psychic process is an image and an 'imagining'[47] . . . and these images are as real as you yourself are real."[48] Or as America's poet of the imagination, Wallace Stevens, has put it: "As in images we awake. . . . It is, we are."[49]

I quote a poet here advisedly, for when Jung uses the word image, he says he takes the term from "poetic usage," "a figure of fancy or fantasy-image."[50] Images are no residues of perception, not decaying sense or after-images—like the copies in naive realism. The image is spontaneous, primordial, given with the psyche itself, an "essential poem at the heart of things."[51] The primary datum is the image—Jaspers' demon—and this is the soul presenting itself, straight on. And, Jung says, libido does not appear as such, but is always formed into images, so that when one looks at a fantasy, one is watching and participating in one's psychic energy. And, he says, these images which are the very stuff of our souls, are the only givens directly presented. Everything else—the world, other persons, our bodies —are mediated to consciousness by this poetic ancestral factor, the image. Whatever we say about the world, other persons, our bodies, is affected by these archetypal fantasy images. There are Gods and daimons and heroes in our perceptions, feelings, ideas, and actions, and these fantasy persons determine how we see, feel, think, and behave, all existence structured by imagination.

This leads to an archetypal psychology: reflection upon the subjective fantasy factors going on all the time, recognition of the images and their ongoing operation in all our realities. As Jung says: "The psyche creates reality every day. The only expression I can use for this activity is *fantasy* ... Fantasy, therefore, seems to me the clearest expression of the specific activity of the psyche."[52]

5. Demons and Daimons

But now you will surely ask, feeling with Jaspers, what about the dangers! Traditions seem all to agree that demons are dangers—as reality of any sort is dangerous. So how can we discern whether these images are evil tempters or guardians? How do we know whether they mean well with us or would possess us?[53] And what becomes of our traditional devotions and observances if we observe the comings and goings of our images and devote ourselves to their cultivation in private active imagination?

These sorts of questions occupied ancient psychologists too. Porphyry, for instance, raised questions concerning distinctions between Gods and daimons, and, like Plotinus before him, criticized theurgic attempts (prayer, divination, sacrifice) to benefit soul by influencing the behavior of daimons.[54]

Iamblichus answered such questions as:"... by what indication the presence of a God, or an angel, or an archangel, or a daimon ... may be known."[55] "What is it which distinguishes daimons from the visible and invisible Gods."[56] His attempts to capture in descriptions and present in an ordered hierarchy[57] the imaginal persons and their effects is comparable in our days with the attempts at precise descriptions of psychic events such as we find among introspectionists, phenomenologists, and asylum psychiatrists. To the intellect, the daimons seem to appear as a pandaemonium, and the intellect's reaction is to attempt an *intellectual diakrisis* (discernment, differentiation). Jung's conversation with the images was a *psychological diakrisis* giving them the opportunity to present their own logos. And, nota bene, they did not appear to him as a pandaemonium, but as distinct, discernable figures with names.

What seems to have particularly occupied the Neoplatonist writers was the relation between Gods and daimons. Jung is not the first to speak of them interchangeably. This occurs already in Homer,[58] and continues almost as a convention. But the distinction is important inasmuch as Gods are supposedly transcendent, daimons immanent, or at least in the middle realm. Thus the distinction involves the more abstract one about distinguishing the forces of the spirit from the powers of the soul.[59] During the influx of emotion or a sudden intuitional seizure how does one tell whether it is a call or a complex, God or daimon? Eventually this simplification, which puts all good with Gods and all ambiguities with daimons, descends into the popular commonplace: is the patient subject for priestly exorcism or psychotherpeutic abreaction? Therefore, the more profound inquiry is the one which attempts to discover the relation between Gods and daimons —or archetypes and complexes to use Jung's language. How do the sudden events attributed to daimons, as well as the images of our interior life, fit within the wider embrace of planetary cosmic principles, the Gods or archetypes?

Proclus resolved this by stating that "about every God there is an innumerable multitude of daemons, who have the same appellations with their leaders . . . because they express in themselves the characteristic peculiarity of their leading God."[60] Implied is that the little daimons of our complexes, symptoms, and fantasies are in the preceding train of the major divinities and that they express, say, Apollonic, Martial, or Venusian qualities. We find the Gods amidst the daimons who surround them. Or as Jung put it: "The Gods have become diseases." We find Gods amid our obstinate 'demonic' psychic problems, if we look with a critically imagining eye. [61]

We cannot here draw the inferences for depth psychology that are offered by Iamblichus. Still, to tempt you to read in him further, let me mention at least the modes of his distinctions among imaginal persons in terms of their beauty, their motion, their luminosity and energy. For instance, he says that heroic *phasmata* are subject to motion and change and show magnificence; that angels do not speak; and that daimons give rise to dread, but their operations are not as rapid as they appear to be.

We return to these early writers for their understanding of the soul, their psychology. They have been turned to too long only for their doctrinal and moral arguments, for their spirituality. In fact, Jung's move has forced the return to that tradition called generally Neoplatonic, because only there did the middle realm of psyche receive passionate attention. (Since 869[62] the main line of official thought had excluded soul by reducing man to a dualist anthropology of body and spirit.) Jung's move also enables us to re-vivify Neoplatonism by relating its insights to the daimons within our contemporary consciousness and the plurality of its worlds.

The plurality of worlds, *psychologically*, refers to the plurality of perspectives that determine our subjectivity, the many eyes that see through ours. For it is not that there are many distinctly different worlds, each ruled by one God; rather, as Kerényi often insisted, there is one and the same world which we partake in but always and only through the cosmos of one or another leading imaginal figure in a particular constellation or mytheme. These are the divine backgrounds to what existential humanism from Nietzsche onward, calls "perspectives". These figures shape our so-called real worlds in the images of this hero, that angel, anima, daimon, or God.

Demonology in its widest sense thus becomes the logos of the imaginal persons who stand within all our ideas and deeds.

Demonology in its widest sense is also *anthropology*, for, as Stevens also writes: ". . . the study of his images/Is the study of man. . . ." [63] Moreover, demonology in its widest sense that includes all persons, even the angels of imagination, becomes a basis not only of our *psychopathology* but of our *epistemology*, of all knowledge whatsoever. Modes of knowing are never altogether purified of the 'subjective factor,' and this factor is one or another imaginal person who casts our consciousness into specific epistemological premises.

Thus the first task of knowledge is knowledge of these premises, or Know Thyself. The pluralities of the imagination precede even our perception of them, not to speak of our understanding of them. ("We are lived by Powers we pretend to understand," said W. H. Auden.) As well, these persons who appear to us as our daimons make possible the modes of our perception and our styles of participation in the reality of things. As first task—and as first enjoyment too—Know Thyself is the self-reflexive moment, a psychological *a priori* within all moments, that laugh of self recognition glimpsed in the images of one's selves in all things.

6. Active Imagination: The Healing Art

We break off here to conclude this chapter with an observation about the intention of active imagination, [64] which Jung links, at the conclusion of his final major work, *Mysterium Coniunctionis*, with Know Thyself. [65] Also, I believe, it is by means of active imagination that Jung joins together again the Hellenistic, Neoplatonic tradition of image-work and the analytical mode of self-knowledge of Sigmund Freud. This connection is more important, I believe, than is the usual separation of Platonism and Freud: for one of the great potentials in Jung's approach lies precisely in making possible a re-reading of Freud.

When we study Jung carefully as to *why* one undertakes active imagination, we find these basic reminders. They can be presented as a *via negativa* of cautions, similar to the sober restraint that imbues Freud's analytical mode with a religious piety.

(1) Active imagination is not a spiritual discipline, not a way of Ignatius of Loyola or of Eastern yoga, for there are no prescribed or proscribed fantasies. One works with the images that arise, not special ones chosen by a master or a code. [66]

(2) Active imagination is not an artistic endeavor, not a creative production of paintings and poems. One may aesthetically give form to the images —indeed one should try as best one can aesthetically—though this is for the sake of the figures, in dedication to them and to realize their beauty, and not for the sake of art. The aesthetic work of active imagination is therefore not to be confused with art for exhibition or publication.

(3) Active imagination aims not at silence but at speech, not at stillness

but at story or theatre or conversation. It emphasizes the importance of the word, not the cancellation of the word, and thus the word becomes a way of 'relating,' an instrument of feeling.[67]

(4) Thus it is not a mystical activity, performed for the sake of illumination, for reaching select states of consciousness (samadhi, satori, unity with all things). That would be imposing a spiritual intention upon a psychological activity; that would be a domination of, even a repression of, soul by spirit.

(5) Nor, however, does this last mean that active imagination is a psychological activity in only the personal sense—for the sake of curing symptoms, calming or abreacting terrors and greeds, bettering families, improving and developing personality. Such would be to demean the daimons into personal servants whose concern must then be with problem-solving those delusions we call realities because we have not seen through to their fantasies, their guiding images that project them along.

(6) Yet, active imagination is not a psychological activity in the transpersonal sense of theurgy (ritual magic), the attempt to work with images by and for the human will. From both sides of archetypal psychology's tradition—Plotinus and Freud—we have been warned against opening floodgates to the "black tide of mud of occultism."[68] Active imagination becomes popularist superstitious theurgy[69] when we: activate the images artificially (drugs), perform it routinely as a ritualism, foster special effects (synchronicities), further divinatory abilities (turning to inner voices to interpret dreams), use it to augment self-confidence in decisions (power). Each and all of these uses are no longer modes of self-knowledge but of self-aggrandizement, now covered by the innocent label 'psychic growth.' Faust still pervades, perverts, our Know Thyself, turning it into a drive beyond the limits which that maxim originally implied: "Know that you are but human, not divine." Active imagination as theurgic divination would work on the Gods rather than recognizing their workings in us. We reach too far, missing the daimons that are present every day, and each night too. As Plotinus said: "It is for them to come to me, not for me to go to them."[70]

So, Jung's method of interior imagining is for none of these reasons—spiritual discipline, artistic creativity, transcendence of the worldly, mystical vision or union, personal betterment, or magical effect. Then what for? What is the aim?

Primarily, it aims at healing the psyche by re-establishing it in the metaxy from which it had fallen into the disease of literalism. Finding the way back to the metaxy calls up a mythical mode of imagining such as the Platonic Socrates employed as a healer of souls. This return to the middle realm of fiction, of myth carries one into conversational familiarity with the cosmos one *inhabits*. Healing thus means Return and psychic consciousness means Conversation, and a 'healed consciousness' lives fictionally, just as healing figures like Jung and Freud become under our very eyes fictional personages, their factual biographies dissolving and coagulating into myths, becoming fictions so they can go on healing.

Therefore, active imagination, so close to art in procedure, is distinct from it in aim. This is not only because active imagination foregoes an end result in a physical product, but more because its intention is Know Thyself, self-understanding, which is as well its limit—the paradoxical limit of endlessness that corresponds with the Heraclitean endlessness of psyche itself. Self-understanding is necessarily uroboric, an interminable turning in a gyre amid its scenes, its visions and voices. [71]

From the viewpoint of narrative, the visions and voices are an unfolding story without end. Active imagination is interminable because the story goes into death and death is endless—who knows where it has its stop? From the viewpoint of narrative, self-understanding is that healing fiction which individuates a life into death. From the imagistic viewpoint, however, self-understanding is interminable because it is not in time to begin with. Know Thyself is revelatory, non-linear, discontinuous; it is like a painting, a lyric poem; biography thoroughly gone into the imaginative act. We may fiction connections between the revelatory moments, but these connections are hidden like the spaces between the sparks or the dark seas around the luminous fishes' eyes, images Jung employs to account for images. Each image is its own beginning, its own end, healed by and in itself. So, Know Thyself terminates whenever it leaves linear time and becomes an act of imagination. A partial insight, this song now, this one image; to see partly is the whole of it. Self-understanding healed by active imagination.

Know Thyself is its own end and has no end. It is Mercurial. [72] It is a paradoxical hermetic art that is both goal-directed and without end, much as the aged Freud, in a last paper before exile from Vienna, said of analysis, both of its end as goal and its end in time: "Not only the patient's analysis but that of the analyst himself has ceased to be terminable and become an interminable task." There is no other end than the act of soul-making itself and soul is without end.

7. Nachklang

A temptation presents itself here at the end—the daimon of the post-script.

The endlessness of the Know Thyself opus is, in Jung's language, a process of individuation. As it goes on, the heat increases. The later, *spirit* operations take precedence, those called distillation, volatilization, sublimation, and particularly what the alchemists call multiplication.[73] While these operations intensify the power of the spirit, they also tend to break the psychic vessel and spill out into matter, action, society, politics, with the fervent urgency of prophesy and mission. With every increase of the spirit's heat, there needs to be a corresponding increase of the soul's capacity to contain it, to amplify within its inner sacral space. This space, this colourful and intricate carpet of the soul, its bordures and silks, is the vessel of the anima—nurturer, weaver, reflector. The *conjunctio*, here, is this contained spirit, this spirited, inspired containment.

The *multiplicatio* is thus not a world-mission, nor is the tincture a direct, naive spreading into and staining with spirit the matters of the political, social world. Rather, I suggest, the *multiplicatio* is an effect of touching all points of the soul, its hundred channels of images, with spiritedness—and of bringing soul-laden imagery by means of which the brilliant impulses of the spirit can find witness and know themselves. Know Thyself here leaves the knower altogether, becoming the spirit's self-knowledge in the mirror of the soul, the soul's recognition of its spirits. The *multiplicatio*, with its hot redness,[74] spreads its own way into the corpus, the body of the world of material events transfusing through the middle realm, the soul or anima. Then these material, political, social events are envisioned themselves as a multiplicity—no longer a dualism of spirit versus matter, calling to dialectical battle. No longer polarity, but plurality. Or, to put it again: Psyche first, then world; through Psyche, the mediatrix, to world, and the world too, psyche, released thereby into many worlds.

3

What Does The Soul Want

What Does The Soul Want
Adler's Imagination of Inferiority

First, he [Eros] is always poor, nor is he delicate and lovely as many imagine him, but harsh and squalid, barefoot and homeless, sleeping on the naked earth, in the streets and doorways beneath the open sky; and like his mother [Penia] he is always in want.

Plato, Symposium 203c

1. Writing to The Soul

"Prudens quaestio dimidium scientiae."

Each psychotherapeutic analysis contains a question, either initiated by the patient or one that I begin to puzzle over about the patient. I wonder what the patient wants, what he is doing here, besides what we have tried to formulate, just as the patient tries to get at what he or she is really coming for. And this question does not occur only on the first day, but recurs, sometimes deliberately reintroduced in order to become more conscious about the analysis. The answers to this question are never as straight-forward as those we might read in books that say the patient wants to be loved, or cured of a symptom, or to find, save, or better a relationship, to develop full potential, or be trained as an analyst. Nor are the wants of the therapist—to help, to be intimate with people, to make money in an armchair, to inquire into psyche, to resolve his or her own complexes —simply all that the question involves.

For what I want and the patient wants seem always to be entangled by another factor, like a thread pulling back, a reflective hesitancy which keeps one's assertions about what one really wants from ever finding direct speech, so that even while broaching one's intentions they negate themselves: "That is not it, at all. That is not what I meant at all."

85

I have come to think that the *uncertainty* about what the patient and I are really there for is in fact what we *are* really there for: this third factor that seems wilfully to keep our aims changing and riddling, and presses the question on us even while refusing our answers.

This moment of reflective intervention, this third factor in the therapeutic experience, I attribute to soul. I believe the patient and I are kept in psychotherapeutic analysis because *it* keeps us there in all sorts of ways, from the obsessions of transference to the intractability of symptoms and the enigma of dreams—none of which phenomena we understand. But most importantly, we are kept there by that sense of wanting something deeply important, which is never identifiable with what we believe we want. Moreover, this inarticulate desire makes us feel a woeful inferiority. We feel inferior because we simply can't grasp why we are engaged in psychotherapy, what it is, whether it is going well or even going on at all, or when it is over. And since we know so little, we rely so much on positivisms, the positive sciences, the positivities of spiritual teachings, the moral positions of ideologies. We clutch at these bright and rigid straws because the base on which we stand, the soul, is endless and unfathomable.

So, to begin with, our theme of inferiority in psychotherapy appears as that want—beyond the actual inferiorities of failure, depression, repetition, and suffering which are the content of therapy—that sense of irremediable inadequacy at the root of our work and presented by the word 'soul.'

One way of settling this uncertainty is to go to soul itself to find out what it wants, independent both of the patient's reporting and the doctor's diagnosing. A direct move of this sort was made already by Tertullian, in his *De testimonio animae*, who wrote

> I call in new testimony, one which is better known than all literature
> . . . more public than all publications, greater than the whole man. . . .
> Stand forth, O soul . . . , stand forth and give thy witness.

The tradition of speaking directly with the soul goes back even further: to the world-weary man in Egypt talking with his Ba, to Socrates with Diotima; and then later there is Boethius in prison, consoled by the voice of philosophy; Poliphilo, among others, in the Renaissance, who converses with his Polia; until finally in our own time the therapeutic method of active imagination, Jung's own example, which we saw in the previous chapter.

Let me show you examples from my practice. You will see how anyone can engage directly in conversations of imagination.

A woman of about forty who worked in a major Zürich bank in a good position, a rural woman who now lived alone in a large modern block of flats, distanced from family, without a lover, and who felt severely this cemented, punctual, secretarial loneliness of her high-standard and competent life—with a secret fear of going insane, of doing something crazy— dreamt of an unknown young man in a white shirt and a green cap who was in prison. He was emaciated, scruffy, and moved jerkily like a mime or an acrobat or "someone who is crazy," she said. In the dream she wanted to get him out of prison.

I said, "Go there in imagination and talk with him."

She found easy access. Unusual, but she did. She asked him questions: his name, where he came from, why he was in prison, what had he done, and what could she do to get him released. He wouldn't talk. All he did was dance jigs and rock his head and act insane. She came to her next appointment, despairing after her visit with him.

I said, "Keep going there. But let's also find out *here* whether there is anything about you that makes him act this way." Then we uncovered that she was "enraged with him:" he was uncooperative; he wouldn't respond and didn't seem to realize that she was trying to help him.

So we began to see that she was the judge, even now judging him in prison when she went to help him, and that her questioning was a further prosecution. It didn't take much for us to grasp who had placed him in jail.

She went back to him. This time she said nothing and he said nothing. They watched each other through the bars. Then in her imagination she found she was inside the bars with him, or at least there were no bars. He now put his head in her lap. She touched his green cap and said, "How are you today?" He didn't reply. She thought, "Aha, I have asked a question again. I am still trying to get information, still being a policewoman." So she let his head stay in her lap with her hand on his green cap. She started to say, "Does this help?" but stopped herself. Then after inwardly parrying several moves of this sort, she suddenly heard him say very clearly, "Thank you. I have been alone so long. I won't go crazy now."

I am sure you have been able to glimpse something of an answer to how to discover what the soul wants. First, we just go to it and let it tell us. Maybe not so easy, for it may not speak until we can listen. Only when she had stopped questioning (prosecuting, inquiring) and condemning (judging); only when she too was behind bars were the bars between them gone; only when she put his head to her lap did his voice clearly sound. And what did he want? Nothing more, it seems, than not to be left alone so as not to go crazy. For craziness (and her fear of it) had been his only means of making his existence known. It had been his defense against her neglect, her judgements, and her terrifyingly efficient rationality.

This next example is from an elderly man, well past sixty, who came from abroad after his wife had died. He had no children. He came to Zürich, took a little room, and began studying everything psychological that he could lay his hands on. He kept a journal. Here is an entry from the journal:

> August 27. Still so cold, I cooked a hot lunch; then back to Neumann. After a while my attention wandered and I heard a clear young voice say, "Where have you been staying, Father?" It could have been the voice of a boy or a girl. If I jump to the conclusion that because of the letter from B, the dream father is dead, then I can now take the father role. I am becoming a father. If it was a boy talking, then is he the divine child in me? Or what? If it was a girl, then presumably she will be an anima figure? But why do I become her father? I am lost. . . . Later: Since the above, I tried to contact the voice with all the most inviting phrases I could summon, but to no avail. Just sit back and love the voice, you old fool. Relax.

I do believe you have felt this man's simple and rather tragic mistake. It is simple because all he would have had to do was hear the child's question—where has he been?—and try to respond to it. And it is tragic in that he answered the voice by psychologisms and interpretations, that is, he used psychology against the soul. [1]

One can hazard that his answer—all those psychologistic questions: because of the letter from B, am I becoming a father, is it a boy, is it a girl, if it's a girl, then. . . —is precisely where he has been staying, and because he has been staying in a puzzling maze of figurings-out, he has not been hearing. The child's voice of simple clarity breaks into the systematic conceptions of his Neumann reading, offering a way out of the maze. But he tries to introspect to the child, and the soul cannot be reached that way, as we discussed above in Chapter 2. Nor, however, can it come forth simply by loving, for his self-prescription to "love the voice" is another psychlogism in this context. The child did *not* say "love me." It asked him, loud and clear, where have you been staying, father. He missed the moment. All his beseeching and cajoling could not bring it back.

How baffling for intelligent, experienced, and mature persons such as these two people were, to be humbled to such foolish inferiority in the face of their own images and voices. How difficult to do right by the soul. It is as if its imagination makes us inferior with that sense of guilt, dumbness, wrongness which happens to a person in therapy, a suffering without pain and without focus, or with wrong focus, where one simply weeps over one's inability, anxious, can't-get-the-hang-of-it, miserably inferior. Perhaps all this happens, not only because therapy takes us back to undeveloped parts or because therapy is a situation of power and dependence. Perhaps therapy invites soul, and soul constellates another, different power that is both our inferiority in itself and also that which makes all we have been and are inferior to it.

Let us look at further behavior of the soul when asked what it wants. This time our documents are letters between a writer and his soul figure named Agatha. The patient had been a successful journalist who had more intelligence and talents than his work had yet showed. He was about to leave his thirties and fell into a depression over aging, the end of the puer meaning the end of giftedness and luck. He was obsessed with the early deaths of Mozart, Pascal, Poe, Dylan Thomas, Nathaniel West, Thomas Wolfe, and other gifted idols, just before forty. His writing was utterly cramped and he was ruled by moods, sprees, and hypochondria. In this condition he began his letters to his soul. Here is the first one:

Dear Agatha,
I have been reading about the anima in Jung and this has prompted me to write you now. I read in Jung that there is an objective psychic world we call the unconscious which we can approach through the anima, in my case then through you. I was intrigued to discover that the anima will sometimes cause moods in a man that he does not understand and even bodily

symptoms. Last night Hillman seemed to suggest that you were trying to come out after having been repressed for twenty years or more. Is this true? Please tell me what you want.

your friend,
William

We have our question: "Tell me what you want." Here is Agatha's reply:

Dear William,

You ask what I want. I need your companionship as you need mine. I want your love and devotion. You must dedicate your life to me and in return I will give myself to you. But you must discover how to come closer to me. I can't tell you that.

You must make the decision yourself. This is also how you can find out about your vocation which has been so troubling you lately.

Since I've seen what you have been doing today, will you permit me to comment on it? You have a good idea to write about, but do it from within. Put soul in your writing. Why not let your imagination run wild again. What you were writing is trash because you don't care about it. It doesn't have value to you. I'll help you.

Love,
Agatha

He answered her immediately:

Dear Agatha,

Thank you for your answer and for your suggestions for my writing. I like your ideas. I want to ask you something else now. What are you up to? I have felt anxious. I want to tell you that I am still frightened about this process. . . . Now tell me, dear anima, what is it that is going on with me? What are you up to?

William

Her answer back was as follows:

Dear William,

I'm surprised at you. Here I went to the trouble to give you all those suggestions for your writing and instead of following them, you turn your back on me and accuse me of causing you anxiety. . . .

One other thing: I'm not anywhere near as dumb as you seem to think. I embody ideals that you value, such as beauty, wisdom and truth. You have been wracking your brains lately to see what you believe, where you stand, what you really value. If you come closer to me it will be easier for you to discover the answers to those questions and to trust your own truth.

Yours always,
Agatha

She signed her letters with love and faithfulness, and called him by his name. He signed his more reticently and often addressed her as 'anima', a psychologism. Their rather formal correspondence went on for some months. But our main point is served if we note again that even when the soul is questioned and answers in good faith, it is not heeded. There is a curious reluctance of the inquirer to submit to its concerns, as if the inquirer has to stay on top despite his best intentions. What soul says is not taken as seriously as what he says; *its* wants come second to his. As the widower was more interested in his psychological interpretations of the voice than in the voice itself, so this writer was more interested in his anxiety and its psychological causes—using soul to clear up his symptoms— than in what the figure told him of *her* needs for companionship and devotion, which of course bore upon his needs for letting go in imaginative writing.

Did you also notice that Agatha wants recognition for her value? She doesn't want to be looked down on as inferior and talked with stupidly. In a conversation with a black snake a woman insulted it by calling it a "fantasy animal." Then later, this snake began to tire of her level of talk. It replied: "I've had enough of what you think, what you need, and what you feel. I'm going back into my jungle and my nature until you come up with a more important question for me."

Our last example for now is from a young intern, a surgeon, Ulrich, making his first attempt at an interior dialogue. He engages a woman in conversation who says:

She: What do you want from me?

Ulrich: I would like to talk to you about the monster in my dream.

She: It is always ready to jump on your back.

Here, an inner voice breaks in, saying, "It is nonsense," a voice of skeptical reason. To this the woman immediately responds by asking Ulrich, "What does it look like?" She is urging: seize the image before the content. Face it; see who is talking or you will be caught by what is being said.

> *Ulrich:* He looks very strict and has a greyish face.
> *Woman:* Give him a name.
> *Ulrich:* I know of no name.
> *Woman:* Give him a name. Any name.
> *The grey man says:* It's senseless to give me a name.
> *Ulrich:* I will call him, The Man.
> *The grey man says:* It's all fancy.

This brief exchange already shows something of what the soul wants. First, it begins by her asking him what he Ulrich, wants, as if in this case what is wanted is that he make clear *his* demands (like the writer who "must discover how to come closer" because Agatha can't tell him that). Then, she also wants our surgeon to be precise, to form an exact image with a distinct name for his internal sceptic. (Notice that the sceptic is only allowed indirect speech.) And, as in our other examples, Ulrich does not quite hear what is wanted. He calls the figure, simply, "grey-*ish*," keeping him vague, and "The Man," keeping him impersonal, distanced, anonymous. Of course, The Man is a symbolic way of speaking about Manhood, the man in the youth; but at this point, by not heeding fully what the soul instructs, Ulrich shows himself in secret league with his inner doubter, his antipsychic sceptic. And so his dialogues with soul ceased almost as soon as they had begun.

My intention with these dialogues is not to draw a general conclusion about soul. I am not using them to make an empirical point, for instance, that this is how the soul speaks, that soul knows what it wants and is infallibly 'right,' or even that the voices I have held to speak for soul are soul. My reasoning in this regard is merely that these are the voices of our images—and as Jung said "image is psyche," so where else hear what soul wants than in the images that intimately speak to our psychic conditions. Moreover, these are the voices of the underworld, those of below, the *inferiores* who speak *sotto voce*, and, this underworld is the preeminent place of soul, as I elaborated in *The Dream and the Underworld.* The *inferiores* are the *daimones* who inhabit the lower regions—shadow is the psychological term;

and we are brought low, humiliated, shamed when these figures speak their wants. This, not so much because they urge dirty-doings, but because we have hidden them away, treated them shamefully, humiliating them by not listening, little caring about the lower reaches of our psychic society.

So these dialogues demonstrate less a hypothesis or even a set of facts, than they show a way of therapy, a method, taken from Jung, of actively being engaged in imagining, and particularly with inferior imagining: images of inferiors and images that make us behave inferiorly—a method quite different from spiritual disciplines that concentrate on higher ideals and goals. Our way, moreover, does not interpret the image but talks with it. It does not ask what the image means but what it wants. So, our first attempt with "What does the soul want?" does not yield a substantial answer, *what* it wants, but a methodical answer, *how* discover what it wants.

The method of inquiry is like writing fiction. Sometimes it is even called "creative fantasy." The genre comes closest to the *Bildungsroman:* an instructive account of many encounters through which the author is educated— here by the soul. Nonetheless, there are differences between fiction writing and active imagination, some of which we have already mentioned. The difference I would like to stress here concerns the active intervention in the fiction of the interlocutor him- or herself. These dialogues demand that one take a part oneself in one's own story, all the while attempting to play the role of the main character, the first person singular, 'I,' as close to social realism as possible, much as Carlos Castaneda, for instance, maintained his guise of social realism by playing the anthropological interviewer in his imaginary dialogues with 'Don Juan.' Even if imagination takes the tale to the Supreme Court, Bedlam Hospital, or the Harem of the Sheikh of Araby, the I is supposed to remain his 'real true self,' passionately engaged yet always a questioner, a fictional figure of usual reality necessary to the style of the story, like the meticulous scribe-author reporting the extraordinary adventures of Adrian Leverkühn in Thomas Mann's *Doctor Faustus.* The task of this usual self is to become educated (or healed) by pursuing its fate, the fate of its soul, persisting with the question, "What does the soul want?" through all the vicissitudes and detours which the imagination creates.

What I would like us most to gain from these documents is the misunderstanding that inevitably occurs. How little we understand the psyche.

Even with the best intentions we seem to bungle—and I quote you subtle dialogues from sensitive persons seriously engaged. There are many others where a person simply starts off by saying, "All right, who are you, what do you want?" as if with gun in hand, finding an intruder in the closet, just plain surly and incurious.

If there is anything we should be skilful with and careful about, one would assume it to be soul. After all, we've been living with it since birth and sleeping with it every night. What could be more important? Yet, were you taking a driving or cooking lesson, you would pay more heed to what was being said than did these persons to their most intimate voices. Therapy pushes for human communications and relationships—but we can't even talk right and hear right with ourselves. Our inner figures, like the snake, glide off insulted. And why, when we do finally hear, almost necessarily do we start off on the wrong foot, all the mistakes, like the old widower telling himself to love when that was not what the child asked, like the young surgeon saying, "I know of no name."

What little we have seen confirms something Jung said: though we all have psyches we are not all psychologists. We are not by nature psychological. Psychology must be gained for it is not given, and without psychological education we do not understand ourselves and we make our daimons suffer. This suggests that a reason for psychotherapy of whatever school and for whatever complaint is to gain psychology—a *logos* of soul that is at the same moment a *therapeia* of soul. We need to gain the intelligent response that makes the soul intelligible, a craft and order that understands it, a knowledgeable deftness that cares for its wants in speech. And if logos is its therapy, because it articulates the psyche's wants, then one answer to what the soul wants is psychology.

Official depth psychology has already declared what the soul wants. That it wants at all is, in the Existentialist school, a revelation of its nature. Its want is the reflection of dread, the hollow abyss on which psychic existence (*dasein*) rests. Upon the soul's want Existentialism has built its Weltanschauung.

If the question is understood in a Freudian sense, then the want of the soul refers to the wish of the id, a desire for libidinal satisfaction. Again, there is constructed a view of reality and of an ego that can minister both to the soul's wants and to a reality that denies its wants.

Taken in Jung's sense, the soul's wants are the ground of psychic pur-posefulness. The soul seeks the initiatory mystery (teleté) which also means fulfillment. The soul's wants are teleological because it is not differentiated, not complete, and not conjoined; the individuation process whose goal (telos) is wholeness answers the soul's wants.

These three examples show that the question we have posed opens into the primary assumptions of depth psychology. We also see that these primary assumptions—dread, wish-fulfillment, wholeness—are metapsych-ological responses to the question of the soul. The voices in the dialogue answer with more particularity, but in each case raising inferi-ority, either as a feeling in the inquirer or as part of the image of the voice. The voices did not provide an overall metapsychological answer, but they did confront us with the immediate psychological relation to the soul in terms of inferiority. In order to come to closer grips with inferiority, which seems so central to our question, let us turn to the history of psychotherapy and more theoretical perspectives. As you might expect, our focus must be on the thought of Alfred Adler.

2. Poetics of Adlerian Therapy

No one who is interested in "psychoanalysis" and who wants to get anything like an adequate survey of the whole field of modern psychi-atry should fail to study the writings of [Alfred] Adler. He will find them extremely stimulating. . . .

C. G. Jung, CW 4, §756 (1930).

Today's student of depth psychology acknowledges Alfred Adler as one of the triumvirate[2] who originated the field—and then tends to leave it at that. There is no Adler archive; no volume of his letters, few photographs, and little mention in the pop-psychology cults. Adler was an Austro-Hungarian from Burgenland (province of Liszt and Haydn), a general practitioner with special training in ophthalmology, a Jew who later con-verted to Protestantism. He was stocky, pale, and rotund with a powerful brow. He served on the Russian front in World War One and lived most of his life in Vienna. He was some fourteen years junior to Freud and five senior to Jung, and himself 32 years old when in 1902 he was invited by Freud to form a small circle of five persons—the original psychoanalytic community. A few years later, 1907, the year which saw publication of Jung's classic work "The Psychology of Dementia Praecox" (CW 3), Adler brought out his classic, *Ueber Minderwertigkeit von Organen* which ten years later in English was called, *Study of Organ Inferiority and its Psychical Compensation*.

The neglectful estimation of Adler's accomplishment is partly due to the man himself whose amiable wit and acute intelligence was either spent in telling jokes, in café conversations, or concealed in a style of writing that both oversimplified a thought and garbled it in the same sentence, whose psychic sensitivity was given to appreciating music and singing, and to tailors, teachers, and social workers—a very different clientele from both Freud and Jung—and whose later isolation, unlike Freud's stoic patriarchal nobility in the face of pain or Jung's gothic stature of towering knowledge, was a harried exile in a New York City apartment during the depression, evenings at the movies instead of the *Schreibstube*, and whose death at 67 was out in the street of a faraway Scottish town. Like his great colleagues, Adler too embodied in his life and death *his dominant ideas: human inferiority and fellow feeling*.

Since the publication of the Freud-Jung letters, these two of the first three remain more than ever in the forefront. The relation between Adlerian and Jungian thought has been especially neglected by followers.[3] Ellenberger's careful and massive examination of early depth psychology has, for instance, only two fleeting mentions of Jung in his Adler chapter. Jung himself was familiar enough with Adler's earlier major works, giving a resumé of their contents in his own writings and paying respects to Adler in many places. During Adler's struggle with Freud, Jung was at first on Freud's side, but then, in a crucial letter (FJL, Dec. 1912, J335), Jung's pen slips, indicating his identification with Adler and independence.

But Jung and Adler have more in common than their battle with Freud. Both Adler and Jung were influenced by Kant and Nietzsche, and both relied upon—though differently worked—such common basic ideas as meaning, individuality, collective consciousness and kinship feeling, opposites and compensation, and psychic bisexuality. If there are Freudian parallels with Jung, even more so are there Adlerian ones.

Adler's work raises into practice that theme of human destiny which is the theme of this chapter as well as a major theme of this book: what do we do with the sense of imperfection? How live it? If there is a primary inferiority in us each and yet the basic human urge is for perfection, how can we recognize our lowness and rise to our heights? Is not this the healing we seek: to be relieved of that double curse in our Western myth—the spirit's vision of perfection and matter's fundamental limitation, two archetypal fictions that have determined even the two senses of a "want," as driving need and as empty lack. And further: what is the connection between the place of fiction in the healing we seek and the place of psyche between the perfections of spirit and the limitations of matter? Adler is that depth psychologist who took these themes—human doubleness, inferiority, perfection, fiction—as basic constructs for his metaphor of human nature.

Perhaps these constructs are better imagined as fictions—if we would be true to Adler. For despite the characteristic dreariness of his style, he is not as literal, as unimaginative as he seems. All his basic constructs can be read as a poetics of life, much as Freud's theory of dreams and Jung's theory of archetypal images are poetics, imaginative undertakings.

a. Organ Inferiority and the Inferiority of the Organic

Already in Egyptian medical ritual there was a relation between specific body organs and specific divine images. In the preparation of a mummy, the lungs were put in an ape-shaped jar, the intestines in a jar with a hawk-covering, the stomach with a jackal's head, and the liver in a human-headed jar. Organs were physically located under the 'headings' of divine images or archetypal structures to which they must have been imagined to correspond or belong. [4] Throughout medieval medicine, owing partly to Galen and to Islam, different kinds of souls—animal, vegetable, generative, spiritual, blood—were attributed to different body regions and systems. In more recent times, Platner (1744-1818) imagined each major organ to have its own vital force, and Domrich, in the middle of the last century, stressed the relation between specific emotions and specific organs. Toward the close of the last century, Wernicke considered the major organs to have

specific symbolic representations. Jung (CW 15, §112; CW 12², §440) refers to Wernicke's idea and, in his Tavistock lectures (CW 18, §135, 299f), makes several
startling diagnostic moves by coupling psychic images and bodily organs. [5]
Freud's theory of character traits that are based in different physiologically
erogenous zones follows a similar line of thought.

Adler's contribution is both more detailed and more general. He argues
that each of us has a place of least resistance, an organic Achilles' heel that
determines the main lines of our psychic life. Of his many examples, Adler
refers "to the degenerative disposition of Mozart's ears, to Beethoven's
otosclerosis, to the stigmatizing of Bruckner's ear," to the hallucinatory
phenomena in Schumann's psychosis, and the suspected childhood deaf-
ness of Clara Schumann (OI, §60). In another example, he refers to a study
showing that more than 70% of students in art schools had optical
anomalies (OI, §61).

Adler makes a one-to-one relation between organ anomaly and psychic
activity: ears-music. That this is far too simple and 'unscientific' was
pointed out to him in the academic commission which unanimously
refused his application for a university Dozentur in Vienna (Ell., 586). His
theory of organ inferiority was not judged scientific enough by the criteria
of the time, first because it considers organs as whole functional systems
related to constitution (which is not the same as heredity), and second,
because it neglects the micro-level of organs and their interrelations.

So, it is not the physiologically literal notion of inferior organs that draws
our attention. Rather, it is the psychologically imaginative aspect—the idea that
one's entire psychological life moves out from a sense of organic weakness
—less an inferior organ, than organic inferiority—that we as bodily creatures are weak in nature, and that it is actually inferiority which goads our
psychic life into action (Lou, §161). In Adler's words: "The realization of
somatic inferiority by the individual becomes a permanent impelling force
for the development of his psyche" (NC, §1). "The inferior organ constantly
endeavors to make a very special demand upon the interest and attention"
(NC, §11). One or another of our organic systems—the throat and swallowing,
the knees and their bending flexibility, the skin and its expressive/protec-
tive sensitivities—becomes the complex or image on which is focussed
one's psychic attention, much as the petite tache humide on the lung of Hans
Castorp was the image source of a magic mountain of psychic activities.

The inferior organ speaks; there is, what Adler calls, an "organ dialect," an "organ jargon," that tells us about ourselves once we learn its language. The afflicted organ gains one's constant attention; like a governing image it "furnishes inexhaustible material" (NC, §7) for one's psychic fantasies and behaviors. So, it is these inferior spots "on account of the introspection and concentration bestowed on them" (NC, §8) that are precisely the places of most potentiality. "All our human culture is based on feelings of inferiority" (L, §45).

We must not take either the locus of the organ nor the feeling of inferiority too literally and narrowly. Adler meant by it also extreme singularities of any kind, including great beauty (OC '67, §473). Nonetheless, the life of the soul derives from and thus requires a feeling of singular inferiority localized in one essential organic image, that locus becoming both a *pars pro toto* for creaturely inferiority in general, and also in particular, an image in the flesh that, like a daimon, guides and guards the actual growth of individual psychic life. We grow around and live from our weak spots. So, any fantasy of cure that loses this sense of organic inferiority, the particular localization in a bodily image also loses, if we follow Adler to his depths, the very sense of soul itself. He says, and underlines, in a letter to Lou Salomé (Lou, §161): *"Psyche is a name for the life-potential* of an inferior creature."* It would seem that to feel a sense of soul at all is to feel inferior. The old search for the bodily localization of soul is now, through Adler, given another meaning: one's soul is one's place of least resistance.

The locus of least resistance is of course precisely where resistance gathers in defense. Where we are most sensitive, we are most stubborn; where we are most exposed, we expend most efforts to conceal. For psychotherapy, Adler's theory of organ inferiority implies that we get closest to soul when we work closely with its defenses. The therapeutic task is not so much breaking down defenses and overcoming resistances as it is one of rediscovering the necessity of these maneuvers which are the psyche's very responses to its weakness. Soul is made out of its own defenses.

Adler's idea of organ inferiority offers several healing insights. First it moves 'the unconscious' from a mental region into the felt experience of inferiority. The unconscious is the immediate suffering of inadequacy, and we are continually producing unconsciousness by defending against feeling inferior. Second, Adler suggests the value of bodily symptoms. Because they remind of inferiority, they keep us in touch with soul. In your symptom is your soul, could be a motto. Third, Adler reformulates the ancient tension between soul and spirit and finds it at work in human life from earliest childhood. The upwards-striving part, historically considered spiritual, puts the other part down, judging itself perfect and its partner, feminine and inferior. The soul is driven by the hierarchical perspective of spirit into regions it considers even more distal and low, the organic body, where the soul makes its presence known as symptoms.

b. Neurotic Thinking and the Hermaphrodite

Inferiority shows itself in our thinking style. Because of feelings of inferiority and insecurity we devise mental constructs to keep these feelings at bay. These constructs act as guiding fictions, governing fantasies, by means of which we apperceive the world. The most basic of these neurotic protections, perhaps the one to which all others can be reduced, Adler calls "antithetical thinking," "which works according to the principle of opposites" (NC, 24ff. 334ff). The mind sets up opposite poles: strong/weak, up/down, male/female—and these guiding fictions determine how we experience. Antitheses divide the world sharply, giving opportunity for exerting power in forceful actions, saving us from feeling weak and incapacitated. More important even than these pairs is that oppositional thinking itself is a pampering safeguard against the true reality of the world, which in Adler's view is one of shaded differentiations and not oppositions (L. §74). For him, to think that abstract opposites reflect reality is to think neurotically, since all antitheses ultimately refer to the power construct of superior/inferior embodied in society as male and female.

Thus antithetical thinking, rather than serving a logic of reality, fosters a magic of power over it; thus it also characterizes the primitive mind (as Lévi-Strauss has since 'discovered' in his binary structure of myth). As Adler says, whether in "mythology, legend, cosmogeny [sic], theogeny [sic], primitive art, psychotic production, and the beginnings of philosophy, . . . phenomena, are sharply separated by abstractive fiction. The urge to do this . . . originates in the safeguarding tendency" (A&A, §248). The "antithesis as set forth in the categories of Aristotle and the opposites in the

Pythagorean table originate also in the feeling of uncertainty. . . . One should not fall into the common error of regarding this as an essence of things" (NC, §25 'PLS A&A, §229). [6]

The ultimate ground of thinking in opposites is the male/female pair, "the only real antithesis" (NC, §99), which in turn can be pushed back to its early childhood experience in "psychic hermaphroditism"[7] (the title of Adler's 1910 paper). "The psyche partakes of both feminine and masculine traits" (IP, §21), and from childhood on we identify not only weakness and inferiority with female, but *also the ambivalence caused by the weakness.* Moreover, hermaphroditic ambivalence itself indicates inferiority and is "apperceived in a strongly antithetical manner," which safeguards us from it (NC, §353). We are convinced by society that "there are only two sex roles possible" (U, §135), and a "dissection" occurs (NC, §345). Uncertainty is met with a clear-cut either/or, that same either/or thinking which Jung connected both with ego-consciousness (CW 5, §§4-20; 8, §557) and with the one-sidedness of neurosis (CW 16, §257; 3, §456).

We may note here that the 'discovery' of the unconscious occurred simultaneously with the 'uncovering' of bisexuality. Ever since then, depth psychology—from Fliess, Weininger, Ellis, and Lombroso to Freud, Adler, and Jung, and then still on to Neumann, the bicameral brain, and fads of androgyny—continues to mix together these two kinds of double natures. Bisexuality becomes indistinguishable from bimentality, so that the two kinds of mental activity are tagged with gender signs, and the self-divided mind is imagined in gender language (IP, §21).

I suspect an archetypal person lurking in this fiction, the very figure Adler named, Hermaphroditus, a figure who both conjoins two genders but also conjoins the main themes of depth psychology: hermetic secrets and hermeneutics with the erotic imagination which sexualizes what it undergoes. Hermaphroditus is a child of Hermes and Aphrodite. It bespeaks an entire mytheme[8] that is at once shameful, libidinal, unnatural, impossibly freakish, and yet draws one into a mystery by evoking insatiable curiosity.

At one and the same time, this figure presents itself in antithetical opposites which are its very essence and yet cannot be taken literally. We are confronted with baffling ambivalences, a prurient knower (the sexual component of the hermeneutic urge) and an incomprehensible unknown (the resistance of the hermetic secret). As repellent as the figure may be, it is yet the child of Aphrodite, ever seductively attractive. Like the hermaphrodite, depth psychology ever holds out riddles for further unmasking, can libidinize without eroticizing, and can transfer fantasy into impossible loves that are not meant for naturalistic procreation. Depth psychology has tried to reduce these phenomena to various rational explanations, but the mythical base is better sought in the figure evoked by Adler.

Not only Adler, but also Freud and Jung seem to base upon the hermaphrodite their visions of the goal of analysis. For Freud this goal is overcoming the fear of castration in men and the wish for a penis in women; for Jung, the goal is expressed in the sexually explicit imagery of incest, a divine marriage, and hermaphroditic *coniunctio*. Only the grotesque image of Hermaphroditus can offer some understanding of the fact that these scientific, sober, and serious ideas are expressed in such peculiar, almost pornographic, organ language.

If restoring psychic hermaphroditism in one way or another is essential to the notion of cure in all three depth therapies, then any disjunctive move is contra-indicated. We may not look to the ego as modelled on the hero, with his sword of decision, to lead us to healing. He is but one more divisive form of the masculine protest against inferiority, and his Oedipus foot, Achilles heel, and Hercules dress are signs of his innate hermaphroditism. Psychic hermaphroditism holds juxtapositions without feeling them as oppositions. Oppositions between conscious and unconscious, masculine and feminine, positive and negative, private soul and public world sever the ambivalence natural to the hermaphrodite. For Hermaphroditus presents an image in which what is natural is the unnatural, a primordial image of *contra naturam*. The physical attitude of natural bodies and biological sexes is revalued by the configuration of non-natural fantasy. Nature is transformed by imaginative deformation, *physis* by *poiesis*.

This tells us what kind of fictions heal: preposterous, unrealizable, non-literal, from which singleness of meaning is organically banned. Is this not fiction per se? Is that why psychotherapy in desperation after centuries of enlightenment turned to myths to find support for its therapy, for without myth the hermaphrodite becomes a sad, strange transsexual, a literal case without a history in fiction. If Asclepius is archetypal figure of the healer, Hermaphroditus is the archetypal figure of heal*ing*, the psychic healing of imagination, the healing fiction, the fictional healer for whom no personal pronoun fits, impossible in life and necessary in imagination.

This figure also helps us re-value the antithetical mode of thinking. It becomes a Siamese-twin mode of insight. One is always never-only-one, always inseparably bound in a syzygy, insighting from a member of a pair.[9] Within these tandems we become able to reflect insight itself, to regard our own regard. Each insight supposes a perspective from which it is seen: whatever appears to me as inferior and weak is viewed from the twin of superiority and strength. Nothing is as such. I can see no mote without at the same time realizing my own beam.

So when we meet antithetical thinking, our question will no longer be how to conjunct, transcend, find a synthetic third, or breed an androgyne. For such moves take the antitheses literally, preventing the mind from moving from its neurotic constructs, from moving from Freudian facts to Adlerian fictions (Lou, §52, §127). Instead our question will be: what have we already done to lose our twin who was given with the soul: the ambivalent, inferior, even shameful feeling of our psychic hermaphrodite. That figure, concealed in 'the opposites' (which are used as a defense against it), is also the figure embodied as goal by therapy in its work—an odd, most unnatural and fantastic, even shameful, work indeed.

c. Fictional Goals

The main damaging movement away from the soul's double nature Adler calls "the masculine protest," the need to win, to come out on top. He also called this the "striving for perfection" or "superiority." At first he conceived for it a variety of bases: social Darwinism and the struggle to survive; biological organ inferiority and the need to overcome weakness; the Nietzschean Will to Power. (At the same time Jung [CW 5] was imagining the movement from ambiguity to directed solar consciousness in terms of the hero myth.) As Adler's thought matured he let go of basing the urge for perfection anywhere other than in the individual human being. It was *sui generis* with human nature, "a striving, an urge, a something without which life would be unthinkable" (A&A, §104). In his late writings, foreground and background are reversed: not inferiority drives us toward superiority, but our inferiority feelings result from the 'innate' urge toward perfection. No longer the fearful soul and its organic weakness compensated by higher spirit but spirit claiming more than soul can realize.

We must take care not to hear Adler only with Jungian ears, assuming that the "great upward drive," as Adler calls it, is the Self as a literal reality.

This is a subtle and important point. Adler says: "The striving for perfection is innate. This is not meant in a concrete way, as if there were a drive ... capable of bringing everything to completion and which needed only to develop itself" (A&A, §104). I believe he is distinguishing between an inherent spiritual finalism that characterizes all psychic endeavor and the fictional goals by means of which the soul images these ideal aims. He warns not to take 'innate' as a literal drive (in a Freudian sense), or as an empirical fact for which we gather evidence (in a Jungian sense). We strive for perfection, but perfection has no concrete empirical goal. Adler might first answer our question—about the wanting soul—by saying the soul wants because its final cause, its *telos*, must remain unfulfilled. Its every movement is innately purposeful and yet it can never enunciate its purposefulness into any literal goal.

Here is the subtlety of Adler's thinking, for his "striving for perfection" is a notion of the spirit that cannot be fixed into any of its epiphanies, even as it imbues all striving with meaning. Here Adler is close to the Jung who considered the final to be a *point of view* toward all psychic events—to look at them as purposeful—rather than to the Jung who tended to literalize the purpose into a demonstrable individuation process of the Self.

Adler could make this deliteralizing move which neither Freud nor Jung could, because he had a source other than theirs: Hans Vaihinger's Philosophy of *As If* (*Als Ob*) to which Adler regularly acknowledged a great debt. (Cf. *IP*, §224, 230; *NC*, passim; El., §606-608, 630-631; A&A, §76-89.) Though Adler is not everywhere able to see his own literalisms as as-if's[10], nothing in his psychology is more characteristic or more valuable for us than is his understanding of the thoroughly *fictional* aspect of our minds. As Vaihinger said, "subjective is fictional" (V, §108). The psyche constructs; it invents images and the mind follows them as its guides; "guiding fictions," Adler calls them.

So, perfection is a necessary fiction, pragmatically necessary just as truth "is merely the most expedient error" (V, §108). When we realize the goal of perfection toward which we strive as an impossibility in every objective and literal sense, then we are also able to recognize how necessary is this fictional perfection. Goals are thrown up by the psyche as bait to catch the living fish, fictions to instigate and guide action. As Jung said, "A spiritual goal that points beyond... is an absolute necessity for the health of the soul" (CW 17, §291). Again, it is not the defined goal, the stated purpose, but the sense of purpose in both Adler and Jung that is fertile. This is the finalistic viewpoint: "there are no purposeless psychic processes," says Jung (CW 5, §90). It all matters, it is all significant. One feels purposefulness, that there is a way and one is moving on a way, a process of towardness, called by Adler striving for perfection, by Jung individuation.

Way in Greek is *methodos*, method. The realization of what Adler and Jung are each talking about is in the way or method of psychotherapy whose own essential purpose is to maintain by its method that sense of way. We can keep this way moving only by keeping purposefulness from becoming literalized into definite goals. Goals, especially the highest and finest, work like overvalued ideas, the roots of delusions that nourish great canopies of sheltering paranoia, those spreading ideals of size and import which characterize the positive goals of so many schools of therapy today. We see enough of the disastrous effect of goals in daily life, where the belief in an overriding idea about one's purpose in life, what one has to do, the *raison d'être* for one's existence turns out to be the very goal which blocks the way. *Psycho*therapy therefore remains with the inferior man, the smaller orbits of ways as goals; perhaps it could even be defined as the method of the small where the small is the way.

Inasmuch as a goal is a guiding fiction showing a way, it is a healing fiction. 'To be healed' is that goal which takes one into therapy, and we are healed of that goal when we recognize it as a fiction. Now the goal as fiction has become a psychic reality, become a psychic reality itself, so that indeed the way did become the goal. This deliteralized method of healing, so ironic, slippery, paradoxical, that seems to fulfill and defeat our striving at the same time (as if the two senses of 'want' suddenly conjoin), bespeaks the mercurial consciousness of Hermes, Guide of Souls, Guide of Ways.

So the best psychotherapy can do is attune the fictional sense. Then the goals toward which therapy strives—maturity, completion, wholeness, actualization—can be seen through as guiding fictions. Then they do not close the way. Therapy becomes less a support of the "great upward drive" than it is a job of deliteralizing the fictions in which purpose is fixed and where one is actually defending oneself against the soul's innate 'towardness' by means of one's goals. This is a therapy of "perspectives" (U, §14). The goals of the spirit do not thereby become illusions to be cynically discounted because they are 'only' fictions. We simply do not hear them in their own literal terms as goals and truths. As fictional perspectives or fantasies they are fecund and expedient, since the value of a fiction lies in the fact that it is a "more conscious, more practical, and more fruitful error" (V, §94).

It seems as if the sense of fiction becomes the goal of psychotherapy and must be the way we perfect ourselves. This suggests that the only possible perfection that the soul can want is perfection of its fictional understanding, the realization of itself in its images, itself a fiction among fictions. Therapy puts the soul through a process which dissolves its substantiations (EI, §608) of itself into perspectives. This method of as-if keeps the way open, and it seems to be where the Adlerian approach comes closest to the religious idea that the final goal is the way itself, in this case, the way of fiction.

d. Gemeinschaftsgefühl

The fourth major component of Adlerian theory is *Gemeinschaftsgefühl*, communal feeling or social interest. "We refuse to recognize and examine an isolated human being" (A&A, §126) because there is no escaping the "ironic logic of communal life" (A&A, §127). Despite the doctrinaire literalness, there remains the subjectivist Adlerian twist, for social interest is not a social *fact* but a social *feeling*, "the feeling of intimate belonging to the full spectrum of humanity" (O'C, §472), *sub specie aeternitatis* (A&A, §142). The iron logic of social embeddedness is not sociologically viewed, but psychologically. It is not merely society comes first, but that the psyche is inherently *mitmenschlich*.

For Adler, not mere circumstances, but their significance (L, §9f) for the individual is his concern, including his social concern. We must bear in mind that Adlerian social interest, from his own early Marxian socialism to his later altruistic idealism, was *psycho*-social, as Freud's concern with sexuality was *psycho*-sexual. Both Adler and Freud were later literalized by minds less subtle than theirs. As it is mistaken to consider Freud's interest to lie in sexuality as such, so it is mistaken to consider Adler's concern to be with society (or Jung's with religion). It is the inherent altruism of the psyche that Adler formulates in his psychology, much as Freud elaborates the psyche's sexuality, and Jung its religiosity.

Thus, social being is a necessity of human being. The fuller and more mature that being, the more this social interest determines a person's behavior and goals. [11] As ensouled beings we feel innately connected with all humankind, past, present, and future. Where Jung demonstrates this universal connection objectively in terms of archetypal patterns recurring through history, culture, and instinct, Adler is concerned with the feeling and activity of this connectedness—how it works in use. How do human beings behave in regard to their altruistic feelings of universal community? The philosophical background here is Kant's ethics, the imperative of human relations.

How in the world knit this Kantian ethical ideal with a Nietzschean Will to Power? Answer: In the world! The seeming conflict between "the two great tendencies," innate Gemeinschaftsgefühl and innate drive toward superiority (UHN, §120) is resolved in Adler's theory by means of an idea of reason also taken from Kant. For a guiding fiction to be heuristically useful and not neurotic, it must be reasonable and reflect common sense, generally valid conclusions about the world as it is. One can be superior only if one is reasonable, which means recognizing social interest so that one's actions are superior from the world's point of view and are useful to others.

Thus a genius for Adler is not a man apart, ahead of his time, a social outcast. "A man of genius is primarily a man of supreme usefulness." "Mankind only calls those individuals geniuses who have contributed much to the common welfare. We cannot imagine a genius who has left no advantage to mankind behind him" (A&A, §153). The ultimate fiction of superiority at the extreme top, the fantasy of genius, is also in service of Gemeinschaftsgefühl. In fact a genius is the one most able to perceive the iron logic of communal life and bring to expression the "general interdependence of the cosmos, which lives within us, from which we cannot abstract ourselves completely, and endows us with the faculty to feel into . . . other human beings" (EI, §609).

So when we ask Adler one more time, what does the soul want? What is its innate intention? We now hear him reply: it wants community. It wants to live with reason in a world that reflects cosmic meaning, then, now, and forever, where the soul as the potential of this order strives with purpose and gives meaning to each act, as if each act 'contributed' to life, moving it toward communal and cosmic perfection. "Contribution is the true meaning of life" (L §14).

But—and the but is big indeed—"the realm of meanings," says Adler, "is the realm of mistakes" (L §9), so that each meaning we attribute to what the soul wants, and he says there are as many meanings as there are human beings, "involves more or less of a mistake." Hence, *what the soul wants* must be a fictional mistaken understanding of every meaning it proposes. This can be the only way that allows human community the very perfection Adler envisions.

We cannot answer the soul's wanting by any certainty, any goal, without realizing at the same moment that this goal is a fiction and that to literalize it is a mistake—even if a necessary mistake. Certainty is an identification with a single meaning; one posits one's own private meaning as a "position of finality" (L §146), which serves only to isolate oneself, defeating our innate altruism and alienating us from the community of humankind. This isolation is also insanity. ("The highest degree of isolation is represented by insanity," [L §184]). Therefore, even Adler's own goal of the community, if taken with literal certainty, can isolate us, as we see in reformers, goodwillers, and terrorists. The more certainly identified they are with their *Gemeinschaftsgefühl*, the more isolated and insane they become. (Yet, in the moment of their defeat and helplessness they empathetically knit into the community which they were trying to dominate). *Gemeinschaftsgefühl* cannot answer what the soul wants or present its goal; it can serve only as an instrument for reflecting all our goals. Do they contribute, do they embody feeling for others? *Gemeinschaftsgefühl* thus offers a mode of discovering our isolating fictions and our mistakes. If we commune at all, it is in the empathy of our mistakes and the humorous tolerance given by the sense of fiction. We are human less by virtue of our ideal goals than by the vice of our inferiority. So the sense of imperfection, Jung's shadow, is the only possible base for Adler's goal of *Gemeinschaftsgefühl*. Jung said the same (CW 10, §579): "Relationship is not based on... perfection... it is based, rather, on imperfection, on what is weak, helpless... the very ground and motive for dependence."

To end with a quote from Jung is to miss the Adlerian twist. The shadow of weakness is not only moral; it is also humorous. The best entry into imperfection is humor, self-irony, dissolving in laughter, the acceptable humiliation that requires no after-compensation upwards. The sense of imperfection may be one way into communal feeling: another surer one is the all-too-human bond of the sense of humor.

3. The Fictional Sense in Archetypal Psychology

(Adler's) individual psychology does not claim to be a system of hypotheses to be checked, but a system of fictions (El. §631).

When Freud (147 §F) in a letter to Jung and Jung (217 §J) in a letter to Freud each say that Adler is not psychological, we can now begin to understand what is meant. Having examined the Adlerian perspective, we are now better able to notice the restrictions on psychology set by Freud and Jung. Without taking Adler into account, psychotherapy narrows its vision and loses a piece of its original ground.

When Freud and Jung used the term 'psychology' they of course referred it to their projects—mapping the deep mind, its invisible levels and dynamisms—in order to account for all surface behaviors of human life from symptoms and opinions to religion and culture. By psychology they both meant: detailed explanatory account of objective but invisible processes at universal levels below individual lives. Freud and Jung were mythmakers, cosmogonists, and the well-known differences between their world constructions were major but not fundamental when compared with Adler's.

For Adler was doing something else—and that alone is remarkable. Imagine being in Freud's tight circle for some nine years, from the very inception of its genius, and being as well within the orbit of Jung's personality, and yet not only devising and maintaining a different psychology, but working from wholly different premises that give a different idea of psychology itself. Adler did not set out to establish an objective system of explanation. He had no regions, levels, psycho-energetics of nuclei, cathexes, conversions, and poles, no peopled cosmology of daimons in the wings. He was not a mythologer.

The differences between Adler on the one hand and Freud and Jung on the other have often been put in terms of different philosophical bases and different sociological influences. Ellenberger makes a more interesting and psychological contrast (El. §889-891). He considers the basic tenets of Freud and Jung to have arisen from within their own experiences during "creative illnesses." Personal, shaman-like visions became the self-validating belief systems which then had to be fortified with empirical verification and the indoctrination of followers (training analysis). Adler's ideas reflect "objective clinical research" (ibid.). Hence, one may surmise, he sought validation less and metaphorical deliteralization more.

I do not hold altogether with Ellenberger here. One cannot say that any one of the three was less objectively empirical or more solipsistically paranoid. For me, Freud and Jung belonged to the prophetic tradition of old wise men in the background of whom moved the archetypal senex. As much as Adler tried to tell us how to live, and what life should mean, his psychology remains subjectivist and hermeneutic. It always returns us to our own fictions, power-drives, and inferiorities. Where Freud and Jung give us meanings, Adler forces us to see through our meanings. As such, Adler is a forerunner of what is now called 'post-modern consciousness,' more so than Freud and also Jung when they pronounce upon the objective nature of the psyche and offer us metapsychological systems of hypotheses. Adler instead has opened the way to psychology as a mode of fiction. As classical depth psychology hardens into orthodoxy, Adler's ideas offer it more and threaten it more than they did fifty or seventy years ago when they were taken as objective *concepts about* consciousness rather than as a *method of* consciousness.

Adler was a *phenomenologist* who wanted to understand consciousness from within itself and without appeal to structures external to it which are always fictions of it anyway (cf. Lou, §43). So, he writes, "The unconscious... is not hiding away in some unconscious or subconscious recess of our minds, but is part of our consciousness, the significance of which we have not fully understood" (A&A, §232f).

What is to be understood, as well as the very nature of psychological understanding itself, is precisely the fictional nature of subjectivity. Then 'unconsciousness' refers mainly to the fact that we are unclear about the subjective fictions that style our lives. In our terms: becoming 'conscious' means to recognize the fantasies playing through all behavior; and the psyche's need for psychotherapeutic understanding means that it asks to become aware of its fantasies.

For example, let us watch how Adler handles that ever-recurring question about the mind: what is its madness? What distinguishes between normal, neurotic, and psychotic? Freud and Jung both deal with this in terms of the subject-object relation and energetics. Both give systematic, dynamic, scientific explanations. Adler gives a *hermeneutic* explanation, remaining wholly within the realm of consciousness and how it intends the world. ("Human beings live in the realm of meanings"—so opens one of his books [L, §5]).[12] Madness is not a matter of energy fixations or withdrawals, past circumstances, uncompensated one-sidedness, conversions into toxins; madness is a matter of interpretation, a delusional poiesis—truly a *mental* disease, a *psychic* disorder, an account of which cannot be put in objective terms.

Adler says: "I readily follow the ingenious views of Vaihinger, who maintains that historically ideas tend to grow from *fictions* (unreal but practically useful constructs) to *hypotheses and later to dogmas.*" "This change of intensity differentiates in a general way the thinking of the normal individual (fiction as expedient), of the neurotic (attempt to realize the fiction), and of the psychotic (. . . reification of the fiction: dogmatization)" (NC, §169 + A&A, §247).

The normal person, says Adler, takes guiding principles and goals, metaphorically, with the sense of 'as if.' "To him they are a figure of speech," heuristic, practical constructs. "The neurotic, however, catches at the straw of fiction, hypostasizes it, ascribes to it a real value." Finally, "in the psychoses, it is elevated to a dogma. The symbol as 'modus dicendi' dominates our speech and thought" (NC, §29-30). What makes madness is literalism.[12a]

Now if the progression from sanity toward mental illness is distinguished by degrees of literalism, then the therapeutic road from psychosis back to sanity is one of going back through the same hermeneutic passage—deliteralizing. To be sane we must recognize our beliefs as fictions, and see through our hypotheses as fantasies. For the difference between madness and sanity depends not on society or politics, upbringing or chemistry, but wholly upon our sense of fiction. Even more: to take literally any of the hypotheses such as upbringing or chemistry, society or politics, as the *real* truth and reason for mental illness is simply mental illness itself, now in the form of an explanatory fiction taken literally rather than heuristically.

But why literalism? This too Adler answers by referring to Vaihinger. Vaihinger observed that the sense of 'as if' involves a "condition of tension . . . a feeling of discomfort which quite naturally explains the tendency of the psyche to transform every hypothesis into a dogma" (V, §125). To be rid of the tension of ambiguity, we move toward the insanity of literalism, and into some kind of action (L, 42).

The acting-out, heroic, "masculine protest" cannot bear the innate tension, elsewhere described by Adler as psychic hermaphroditism. Here we feel close to our inferiority. This is the condition of tentativeness, where our hypotheses feel less certain and positive and our beliefs are vulnerable. If we can stay with this condition of ambiguity we are less able to be literal about anything, and so less likely to move into the delusions of neurosis and insanity.

Thus psychic health requires remaining within psychic hermaphroditism, because it constellates those feelings of inferiority which prevent literalism. The image of the hermaphrodite keeps the tension. Modern Adlerian therapy[13], which emphasizes humor and paradox (the Adlerian junktim[14]) as modes of healing, reflects the odd and uncomfortable figure of the hermaphrodite, an image which like humor, like metaphor, prevents antithetical literalism. Adlerian therapy too calls upon metaphorical awareness, ourselves translated out of singlemindedness, all positions figures of speech whose very words are de-literalized as in a joke or poem. We can take nothing positively without losing the feeling of inferiority, and thus inferiority is a key to the psychological, metaphorical sense of reality. Now the poetic becomes the practical, and the positive, insane. We look at life with the poetic eye: "Understanding a style of life is similar to understanding the work of a poet. A poet must use words; but we must read between the lines" (L, §47).

This penetration into the Adlerian psychology of psychic health and madness will tend to be considered a non-psychology by Freudians and Jungians whenever they take their guiding fictions too literally. When Adler states that "one must avoid taking the sexual fiction, this, so to speak, 'modus dicendi' or as I have called it, the sexual jargon, for an original experience" (NC, §158), (that is, literally), then Freudians are obliged to review their meta-psychological doctrine of sexual libido. If in Adler's view, private worlds and antithetical thinking are neurotic manifestations, then Jungians are obliged to review their doctrines of introversion and opposites. If Jungians and Freudians are unwilling to set all their hypotheses into the as-if mode, they are losing touch with the inferior tentativeness of all psychological statements, losing touch with soul itself, and are relapsing into a therapy based on neurotic defenses that have been raised to positive theoretical principles.

We have now embarked upon an Adlerian critique of psychotherapy. We do this on the constant base of our first question, what does the soul want? Having assumed that the soul speaks with the voice of the *inferiores*, those kept down, below, and behind, as the child, the woman, the ancestor and the dead, the animal, the weak and hurt, the revolting and ugly, the shadows judged and imprisoned, then it will be the task of any *psycho*therapy to stay in touch with and be moved by these *inferiores*.

But we saw from Adler that there is a passionate desire to leave inferiority behind, thereby develops neurosis. Therapy too can become neurotic when, by means of its literalized fictions of doctrine and profession, it safeguards itself from its necessary feelings of inferiority. Then it too loses consciousness even in the name of consciousness. It then runs the risk of becoming not a therapy of soul for soul, but an activity of private worlds, called 'analytic schools,' developing a life-style to stay on top of the soul.

In the last ten years or so a critique of therapy has been emerging among some Jungian psychological thinkers in various places, occasionally under the common name of archetypal psychology, whose writings show approaches remarkably similar to aspects of Adlerian thought as I have been presenting it here. I would like to review their work, which is an added pleasure for me since they are colleagues and friends.

Wolfgang Giegerich in Stuttgart has been carrying the examination of fictions directly into theory itself. He has attempted to show that neurosis is not merely a condition which a patient has and therapy cures, but that it is fostered and hardened whenever the psychological concepts within which therapy is set remain unexamined. Healing, and cure, positive and negative, ego and the unconscious, matriarchy and stages of development, are not literal 'reals,' but heuristic fictions or fantasies which must be recognized as such if psychotherapy is to keep connected with what Giegerich calls "the neurosis of our own discipline." "Psychology itself must be its own first patient" (Spr '77, §168).

A similar appeal for maintaining contact with inferiority in psychological theory is presented by Mary Watkins[15] at Clark University. Her focus has been on methods of active imagination. She shows that neurotic concepts are at work in the very therapies aimed to cure the neuroses. What turns up most frequently in the instructions for working with images in interior space is the attempt to dominate and exploit the lower, darker, weaker, and uglier psyche for the fictional goals of ego-superiority. We ask not what they want, but what our ego wants. Her work bears out a basic archetypal attitude that we also find in both Adler and in Jung: the individual is in a larger context of psyche, of Gemeinschaft, so long as he imagines the soul a private interior of his 'own,' so long will he naturally believe he can dominate its space with his intentions.

In Zürich, Adolf Guggenbühl-Craig in a brief and fundamental work[16] has developed the idea of antithetical thinking along the lines that also can be called Adlerian. His focus too is Adlerian: power, the move towards superiority in all helping professions and the polarization into weak and strong (patient and doctor, pupil and teacher, etc.). This destructive antithesis occurs, he says, when the doctor loses touch with his own vulnerability, the teacher with his own ignorance, and the social worker with his own asocial immorality. Help and healing depend altogether, in Guggenbühl's view, upon maintaining the shadow awareness of inferiority.

Another Jungian psychiatrist in Zürich, Alfred Ziegler, works in the field of psychosomatics and mechanical dream research. His studies (cf. Spr '76) pick up another theme of Alfred Adler: organ inferiority. Ziegler reads from his examination of dreams and those symptoms called 'psychosomatic' that our suffering is psychophysical and sui generis. Dreams statistically show more displeasure than pleasure; the body is chronically inferior and incurably immune to the guiding fictions of symptom-free health and positive, life-enhancing, nature. Our feelings of inferiority bespeak the fundamental organic inferiority of the human psychophysical being which can only exist in a state of relative discomfort in order to maintain the tension base of its consciousness. From this viewpoint, loss of the sense of organic inferiority is not only delusional, but suicidal.

Another of Adler's notions, psychic hermaphroditism, has been a main subject for Rafael Lopez-Pedraza in Venezuela. In seminars at the University of Caracas he has been elaborating the kind of consciousness, presented in the myths of Hermes (op. cit. sup.) and also of Psyche and Luna, which never lets go its weakness and which remains ever at the borderline, not separating into antithetical literalisms of male and female, good and evil, progress and regress. These are permissible only as guiding fictions to be judged wholly by their therapeutic use, their effect on soul. He has been working out an archetypal base for consciousness in mythic figures, especially Hermes, altogether different from the Promethean ego and its necessary oppositions and literalisms.

In several papers[17] on the Goddesses, Gaia, Demeter and Persephone, Patricia Berry has plunged the notion of inferiority to archetypal depths, to that emptiness within the image of the maternal and material itself. The supportive ground of being is by nature and essence lacking, always wanting, a wanting which psychotherapy attempts to overcome with various sorts of substantiations in practice and theory. Her work offers a new approach to inferiority and extremity, a way of reduction or leading back to the void as substance itself, so that psychotherapy need not be a defensive system against the necessary pathologies or soul-suffering that opens us to deeper ground.

At Sonoma State University, Gordon Tappan (who was once in fact an Adlerian and then a Jungian) has taken the further step of combining inferiority feeling with social feeling in graduate education. His innovative degree program in archetypal psychology depends on his role as therapist-educator within a social group. He follows one of Adler's life-long interests, education[18], in this case putting into practice the fundamental need of soul for mind and mind for soul. His work, bringing together academic discipline with individual image, attempts to heal the division between the logos of psyche and its therapy.

Then at the University of Connecticut, Charles Boer and Peter Kugler (Spr, '77) have been advancing a theory of perception which demolishes—as Adler too tried—the notions of private worlds in the mind, private unconsciouses and privately experienced images. Their theory returns importance to the world in the street as it is immediately imagined.

This return of psychology to the street is the main concern of programs initiated by Robert Sardello at the Dallas Institute of Humanities. His primary metaphor, City, enables the pursuit of Adlerian social and educational interests into a deeper cultural psychology. By examining the phenomena of our daily urban life by means of a metaphorical and imaginal approach, his studies relate the soul of the city with the City of the soul.

Too, there is the work of Paul Kugler on organ language, the words in the body which turns body into verbal image. Kugler makes us reach further toward the idea that our guiding fictions are found best in *modus dicendi,* the words which "dominate our speech and thought" (Adler), therewith opening a new approach to the poetics of psychosis, the innate insanity in language when taken by the letter.

Time limits this survey—an exposition of my *Gemeinschaftsgefühl*—to bare remarks about a few persons only, yet I cannot pass by without mentioning the significant work of David Miller and Rudolf Ritsema. Of Miller's many and complex contributions[19], I want to single out his method. For it is less his assiduous scholarship, the research and ideas drawn from it, but the simultaneous deliteralizing of the scholarship and ideas by means of Adler's "junktim," the metaphor, the verbal juxtaposition, off-reversals and odd-combinations of thoughts, fields, and periods, especially through humor, that allows a sense of fiction to shine through every sentence. His style opens into a psychotherapeutic method of intellect because it is a seriousness that prevents the ego's literal earnestness. He attempts a *poiesis* of the borderline trying to keep the mind from breaking into divisions called sane and insane.

Rudolf Ritsema's examinations of the *I Ching* (as published serially in *Spring* since 1972) have furthered psychological insight even into our Western language habits, where the literalist fiction is most invisibly embedded. Ritsema shows how to stick to the image when using words. His "syntax of the imaginal" defeats those mental habits which rely on causality and linear thinking, positivity of statement, dogmas—the very progress to insanity that Adler warned of. Ritsema's scrutiny of the *I Ching* also implies that those two totem poles which guard the approaches to psychotherapy like dumb stone giants from Easter Island—I mean The Masculine and The Feminine—are modern monolithic concretisms, a pair of substantiated neurotic antitheses that can draw no support from the flowing play of Yin/Yang images, always subtle, differentiated, and precise.

The work of these friends, as well as my own recurring essays on failure, depression, betrayal, suicide, woundedness, abnormality, ageing, and my

J

orientation from the underworld, may help convey a current in contemporary psychotherapy grounded within experiential inferiority. In a sense, we are like the Taoists of psychotherapy, staying with the low, dark, and weak, staying with the inferiority of the discipline given with the lowness, darkness, and weakness of the soul.

From another perspective our work is like Zen in its attempt to see through the subjective fictions of consciousness (EI, 624), to dissolve those literalisms with which consciousness identifies and then names as the methods of becoming conscious: thinking in opposites, inventing private worlds of individual subjectivity and objective systems of concepts to account for these worlds, or fiction-ing goals and their accompanying optimistic feelings. Our Zen is on the watch lest the concepts of psychotherapy and its theories of invisibilities cover the stark presence of soul.

4. The Communal Sense

> The only feature common to all mental disorder is the loss of *sensus communis* [common and communal sense] and the compensatory development of a *sensus privatus* [private sense] of reasoning.
>
> Immanuel Kant

Now we return to our original question about the soul's wanting and to actual dialogues. In these, the difficulties of listening to the soul seem less to stand in the way, so that we have a better chance to hear its wants.

The first example comes from a young, divorced teacher, a German woman who lived with her daughter. She embodied a vigorous animus development in Jung's sense, or a masculine protest in Adler's. Her own daughter did not carry her soul values because her daughter was too much like a younger edition of herself, an adaptive, go-ahead little girl. Instead there appeared another little girl in her fantasy, an as-if daughter, dark with big eyes such as one sees on famine posters and save-the-children appeals. Sometimes this little girl was also a little boy, between 7 and 11: the psychic hermaphrodite. We enter the conversation just where our question is being asked. The woman says: "What do you want then?"

Child: To be let be, and never have to do anything. You are always pushing me around.

Woman: I want you to grow up.

(Do you notice that we have already switched to what the woman wants. The child is on the defensive.)

Child: What's better about that?

Woman: Then you won't be such a sick drag.

Child: If I have to grow up for your sake, I won't.

Woman: Stubborn!

(The woman writes: I was furious (*rasend*) and breathing very hard.)

The Child starts to cry. Then it says, "Teach me. I don't know how. I want to learn." (With this the woman suddenly finds herself sobbing, for she is after all a teacher. She said she was crying "not as a child but as herself." She realized that this child of her soul was why she was a teacher—by vocation as well as profession.) The next evening she returned to the dialogue:

Woman: First you said you want to be let be and then you say teach me. I don't understand you.

Child: You don't understand me.

Woman: If I let you be, I'm not teaching and if I'm teaching I'm not letting you be. I don't know what to do with you.

Child: You don't know what to do with me.

Woman: You make me feel stupid. I never feel more inferior than when I'm with you.

Child: Good, now you can teach me.

Woman: I still don't understand.

Child: When you understand you can't teach me because then you don't respect my ignorance. For you, understanding me has equalled pushing me around. Please teach me things you know, things you read. Teach me psychology, about psyche. I want to learn to think, to understand, and not how to behave.

Let me point out here the close interplay between thinking and feeling. They are not antitheses. Here, feeling for the child is teaching it to think. I can also point out the Adlerian content to this dialogue: only when she becomes inferior to her inferiority does the therapy of that inferiority, the child, begin. But my main intent with this piece of soul fiction or active imagination is to show the relevance of psychology for psychotherapy, that the soul wants to learn psychology, wants thoughtful formulations of itself, and that this is a mode of its healing. This woman listened. She began to read psychology differently, not learning it for information to apply it to education, or to become an analyst, but in connection with her experience, especially in connection with her inferiority, her weak and dumb child.

I'd like to read several more pages from other persons illustrating this desire of the soul for psychology, for psychological wit and intelligence, for heightened, accurate, penetrating use of mind. Sometimes, the soul figure says, "Don't be so silly," or "Use your intelligence," or "Stop all this talk and think what you are saying!"

Our next example from a man in England took place some years ago, after the war. This man had been wounded, having lived a heroic military sort of life as a British Colonial. He had suffered a wound in his left shoulder and his heart was affected. In imagination he has just begun dialogues with a deformed and hunchbacked black woman, who called herself Sheba.

Sheba: I can't bear for you to see me. Why did you come. I can't bear it. Go.

Mark: How could I. It's like asking me to leave my heart and left arm.

Sheba: I am your heart and left arm. That's how my crooked back appears in you.

Mark: The Jap hit you at the same time, is that it?

Sheba: You were brave.

Mark: A compliment from you?

Sheba: You *are* brave.

Mark: Can I touch you. (He writes: Sheba is standing naked in a light-green room. She is abysmally deformed: doubled over on herself, the back of her head slightly lower than the high point of her hump. She is black. Her body is very thin with some traces of a former beauty. He approaches her, touches her hump, and slowly caresses it. She weeps.)

Sheba: They should never have let you in. Leave me, leave me.

Mark: I'll be back.

(He does leave her as *she* wants, showing a remarkable sensitivity as to when to break off. The next day, he walks with her along the actual Thames Embankment, talking as he walks and noting it down later.)

Sheba: I've never been out before.

Mark: Never?

Sheba: Not like this. . . not on my own. Only in the jumble of another woman's being. Her being melted into mine, except when I wanted to drive her away from you. Or you from her. . . (she becomes breathless during this passage). Slower please.

Mark: (Dropping to a slower pace) All right?

Sheba: Still too fast. It's the first time you see.

Mark: (Walking as slowly as he can) All right?

Sheba: If I'm to be with you, sometimes you'll have to slow everything down—walking, thinking, talking.

(They come to heavy, quickmoving traffic at a corner.)

Sheba: Oh, I'm scared.

Mark: Easy. It's all right. How do you like it (as they cross the road together)?

Sheba: You won't be able to understand me when I say that this is the happiest moment of my life—just out walking with you.

To take the soul into the street, and taking care of it in the street, not in the jumble of another person's being, not in private in one's interior dialogues and emotions. But psyche into life, as one goes along—was the Solomonic wisdom taught by this Sheba.

A characteristic of this dialogue appeared earlier in Ulrich's, the young surgeon's. When the emotion gets very close, then there is a lapse into indirect speech, as if the ego-person tries to distance from the imaginal intensity. In Ulrich's case it was the greyish man whom he did not let speak directly; in Mark's case it is the moment of seeing Sheba naked, black, and deformed, the moment of touching her body.

Their relationship in the world, the street, and the body reconnected Mark not only with his loss of soul (anima) "in the jumble of another woman's being," and in his too-fast pace, but also with his physical courage, his heart to live. Adler said that courage without a goal is quite useless. Sheba, by mentioning Mark's bravery, restores to him the courage he had had during the war, when goals were easy. She now connects courage with her, his dialogues in soul-making. Their entire encounter, including their walk in the street, constellates the bravery it takes to meet the crippled ugly soul and to take one's inferiority as seriously as the heavy traffic on the street.

The fuller, more philosophical implications of the dialogue between Mark and Sheba are better presented by our final excerpt, this time from an eclectic psychotherapist with wide experience who came to Zürich for some deeper Jungian training. Again our refrain:

He: What do you want?

"I want out," says a voice he called variously "soul-voice," "anima," "chest-voice," "my person."

He: Out! That sounds like you are a prisoner.

Soul-Voice: I did not say that. I am not blaming you. You keep me, for better or for worse, inside. Protective. But I want out.

He: I do not understand [that same sentence!]. It has taken me so many years first to find you and get you inside, as a psychological factor as Jung says[20], so we can have dialogues like this, that to let you out means to start all those projections once more.

Soul-Voice: You are afraid to let me out, then you are keeping me for worse: not protecting me, but yourself. I *am* a prisoner.

He: Just wanting to keep you inside and psychological makes you a prisoner?

Soul-Voice: A prisoner in your psychology. You have imprisoned me in your psychological system, preventing me from appearing wherever I please.

He: It's the way you say that, that makes me afraid: "wherever you please" means anima attractions, foolish business speculations again, wild goose chases. When you are 'out' I become a silly goose. I can't afford it. I must protect myself.

He was dissatisfied with this warring state of affairs, himself as warden of his soul. She left him perplexed. On the one hand he did not feel adequate when she had her way; on the other hand when he had his way, he became hard and oversure. He tried to find a mode that was softer and more malleable and at the same time not so vulnerable that he had to cover-up and close off. Two days later he turned again to the dialogue:

He: I was too hard with you. I did not listen. I interpreted and told you my fears.

Chest-Voice: That's all right. There is no hurry. I like your mistakes.[21]

He: Even with you?

Chest-Voice: Each time you make a mistake you get nearer to me, and we can get clearer. You are at your worst for me when you are on top. [Note

again the Adlerian idiom.] You know by now that you used to find me
only when you were sick or had your heart symptoms.

He: But my mistakes are the very ones that keep us apart. I mean like this
one which always interprets and doesn't listen.

Chest-Voice: It doesn't matter so much, as long as you sense that your
mistakes have to do with me, that it bothers you, eats you, that whatever happened last, like two days ago, preys on you. That's why I like
analysis, and why you are a good analyst. It keeps you worried, uncomfortable, like a little gravel in your shoe. You're a little bit hurt at every
step.

He: May I go back to my question?

Chest-Voice: Sure. You don't need my permission. That's another mistake.
Just talk with me. What's on your mind. Don't be so gingerly.

Do you notice how difficult it is even for this sophisticated analyst to find
the right 'speaking terms' with the soul. Do you see how submissive and
inferior he becomes, just as others become dominating. Now we come to
the more philosophical part concerning the soul's intentions.

He: My question is—what do you mean by wanting *out?*

Chest-Voice: To be the large to your small. As long as I am in—in your
interior, in your psychology, in your projections—I never come to full
stature. You still have not recognized me.

He: But aren't you supposed to be inside? My interior person?

Chest-Voice: You are stuck in words. Interior simply means deeper. Going
inward simply means going more deeply into things, into their heart and
soul. Interior is a sense of inward chambers, the hollow in the chest that
resounds. It isn't a place to go and it doesn't mean all those things you've
learned and taken so literalistically: introverting, introspecting, internalizing.

He: I don't know what to say next.

Chest-Voice: Then don't.

More than a week passed before he took it up again, although he had been
struggling with her "wanting out" without resolution. In fact, *he* did not
take it up again, for it happened to him after swimming in the lake. On
coming out of the water, he experienced his body wrapped in space that
was full of presence, an air that had a density. He heard her say distinctly,

so aloud that it was as if an hallucination: "Now I am out. Now you are in."

When he told me this I remarked about the *coagulatio* of the soul in alchemy; its becoming thickened, sensed as a presence. This had evidently happened like a chemical process. After long cooking, stirring, and containing, suddenly, as in making a sauce, a coagulation takes place.

The conversation between them then went as follows:

He: I get it now: all these women, all these things I have been into, that you, anima, have led me into, that I have called projections, have been to give me the sense of being in, of being smaller than, inferior to what I have got into. That's why it has always been too much. That's the secret of anima possessions: to show me that you possess me and are bigger than me. If I can give you this recognition, . . . no, if I can keep this awareness of my inferiority to soul, that I am always somewhere embraced in a psychic state, then I don't need to be possessed to be proven that I am embraced.

Anima-Voice: I can't guarantee anything. I do not obey the law of compensation. That would be to put me back inside something.

He: Then it is just feeling your presence around me.

Anima-Voice: That is not a 'just.' And it is not a 'feeling.'

He: What is it then?

Anima-Voice: It is being. Being in the soul.

He: Is this what you want, what soul wants?

Anima-Voice: Out; everywhere; space.

He: I move in your space.

Anima-Voice: I move you in our space.

He: Our space? You move me?

Anima-Voice: My images move you and unless you move, swimming through the water, you do not sense the space. The space of the soul comes into being only through your movements—not only those movements of arms and legs, but the movements of the mind and heart. Yes, the heart's symptoms too. Unless you act, do, behave, think, live, wish, desire, imagine, I am empty. I am nothing unless you move in me, as my content. You are the place of my psychic activity; but do not enclose me in the activity. The soul is never the same as its actions. I am not behavior but the image in the behavior. However, do not try to take me out by extraction from the behavior. I am independent of every place you try to put me and wholly dependent on moving in and out of those places where I am kept. My spaciousness depends wholly on moving out.

This dialogue is witness to the philosophical dimension of soul. It reminds us of a *récit* in Corbin's sense. The material is worthy of ancient writers for it takes up the ancient problems. Anyone familiar with the history of psychology will recognize Heraclitus re-emerging for how can a soul which is without limits be held 'inside' a paltry person? One will recall the instructional style of Diotima teaching Socrates, will remember Plotinus' insistence on the free movement of soul through many places in an individual's consciousness as well as its inherent relation with images, and will recall Augustine's wrestling with the inner-outer, larger-smaller problem in his *Confessions*. Even a shade of Aristotle rises in this dialogue, the Aristotle who considered soul to be prime mover, its movements being our life.

One will hear also Jung who said "image is psyche" (CW 13, §75), who said that consciousness comes from the anima which is the life behind consciousness from which consciousness arises (CW 13, §62; CW 9, i, §57), and who also said "man is in the psyche."[22]

However, and here is the rub, the actual effect of this dialogue on the patient was not philosophy or imagination, or even a further exploration of his internality. Our man moved in the direction of Alfred Adler.

He found the political and social world. When he went back home, he gave up practicing group-therapy, considering it a compromise because it did not let the soul truly out. Instead, he joined actual groups with social aims—a medical insurance-reform group and an environment-protection group. He began teaching a course in night-school, accepted a volunteer job in his professional society, and yet still carried on his individual psychological practice. He found what Adler considered the only realistic goal of psychotherapy, *Gemeinschaftsgefühl*.

Now Adlerians say that *Gemeinschaftsgefühl* can "not be brought into existence by a conscious decision in rational terms" (O'C '76 §15). It won't work to urge ourselves to get involved. There must be a shift in cosmos so that one actually feels an expanded sense of identity. Adler writes:

> To hear, see, or speak 'correctly' means... to become identified with him or with it. The capacity for identification alone makes us capable of friendship, love of mankind, sympathy... [and] is the basis of

social interest (A&A, §136) which may extend beyond... towards animals, plants, lifeless objects, or finally towards the whole cosmos (U, §43).

We watched this shift of identity happen. The voice called 'anima' or 'my person' and at first located in the privatissimum of his chest gave our patient that intense sense of personal identity leading him to cling to soul as his own private interior event. Ownership. But such interiority breeds inferiority: it inside me; it small, me big; it within and below, me on top and containing. The movement we watched was from *my* soul to *the* soul, from *my* anima to *anima mundi*, from subjective feelings to objective world ensouled. Remember how the soul voice refused to be considered as merely his feeling.

The process of releasing soul from literal interiority goes hand in hand with coagulating it. As long as it must be kept, then it is imagined to be delicate, fragile, winged, a vaporous pressure always wanting to fly out and disappear like a nymph into the more solid form of another person. If we keep the soul so carefully, are we not pampering it as an invalid? Are we not further separating psyche from common life in the street, depriving soul of community and community of soul?

Adler warns against literalizing the communal feeling into a specific community with specific goals. *Gemeinschaftsgefühl* "is never (only) a present-day community or society, a specific political or religious formation." It means community "under the aspect of eternity" (A&A, §142). Although our man did move into actual social service, he saw this not in terms of the goals of these services, but these services as places where an expanded chest of sympathy could live and breathe.

If we ask how did the shift of identity come about, and therefore ask more deeply how does social interest itself come about (since it cannot occur through conscious decision), then we discern a myth at work making possible the capacity for identification. This man's prolonged engagement with soul led to love. Psyche led to Eros. We are returning to what I tried to present in *The Myth of Analysis*: the relations between Psyche and Eros as the dominant myth of psychotherapy.

Our example shows that he did not first love soul and then move his love to the world as a moral[23] duty: to do unto others. Nor was it that soul first loved him so that he could return this love to the world. The love itself changed its nature, as in the myth of Eros and Psyche. Now it was no longer his loving the soul or caring for it in *Sorge*, as an *Ich* vis-à-vis a *Du*. Now

Psyche and Eros had come together indistinguishably: when he was with psyche, there was love that included him as one of its images and expanded 'out' of its own accord into fellow feeling. Through feeling the importance of his psychic persons, he felt loved by them. There was no longer some one, a subject, loving some one else, an object.

It was not love of world that led him to world but love of soul, because soul, as *anima mundi*, is itself world, the place of soul's making. The indirect passage of love to world via soul is processed through the multiple erroneous labyrinths of psyche. Mistakes, Adler might say, turn love psychological, that intelligent, differentiated understanding of the identity of what is loved. We can only identify 'correctly' when we can recognize the identity of each face in its unique image.

The work our patient did with his patients and in political committees required an acute sense of loving that was simultaneously a sense of psyche. He was dealing not in humanistic principles and sweeping mystical feelings, but in the art of the small, individually different particulars. Persons. (Individuation, says Jung, means differentiation.) That love is differentiation was also made clear to him in one further dialogue with which we shall conclude.

He starts off: I can't see the trees for the woods. Ever since I have felt wrapped by your thick presence, I feel submerged. I guess it's like the lake experience.

Voice: Or the womb. Ontogeny recapitulates phylogeny: soul-anima returns first to mother-anima. You are re-connecting to the sources of all life. Immersion in your own chest.

He: I seem to have lost my own space by being in yours.

Voice: Then make place for yourself.

He: So you do want an ego.

Voice: You are interpreting again. I said, make place for your self. I said nothing about ego: Who is that? You want to know what the soul wants; now you know, in part; it wants you to make place of space.

He: I get it! I have been spacey, all over, swimming without structures, without hierarchy, without knowing what belongs where with myself or anyone, unless I can place things.

Voice: Yes. It is not a question of giving space to others, or feeling their space, your patients, but of perceiving the exact place where they each are at, where they move within, what part of the house is theirs, accurately and small. Place qualifies space. The canvas is made of small soft brush strokes, the sculpture of chipping, the symphony of tiny notes. Molecules, each at an exact place. Each image is a placing. You can't move small enough.

Her instruction has begun to be sibylline, and we break off here because working out her statements took him more time than we could ever have at our disposal. But we can conclude this about our starting question:

The soul wants many things—to be loved, to be heard, to be named and seen, to be taught, to be let out, out in the street, out of the prisons of psychological systems, out of the fiction of interiority which forces it to project itself to gain outer recognition. We know too it has a vital interest in the life and behavior of its keeper on whom it depends; but this interest is not in the life and behavior as such, to help it or cure it. Rather it seems to be an interest in life for soul's sake. It seems to ask that our sense of first importance shift from life to soul, that life be given value in terms of soul and in preference to a soul valued in terms of life. Thus, it does not brook neglect in life—this above all; and so it is like the ancient Gods who considered impiety to consist in one great sin, neglect.

We also saw that there is in the psyche a living interdependence between its logos and its therapy. The psyche asks for psychology as necessary for its therapy and it asks for psychotherapy in order to make its psychology. Even if the soul is wary of imprisonment in this logos, in literalized structures, systems, words, it is yet profoundly philosophical. As we saw, it philosophizes. Psyche is an intelligence that wants an intelligent psychology in response. Its native inferiority does not imply stupidity; it cannot live on the clichés of inferior psychology or even on the superior ideas when simply taken over from masters. Remember the voice that said, "I like your mistakes;" the voice that said, "I obey no laws of compensation." The psyche's therapy wants one to work out the psyche's logos, each individual a psychologist.

Psychology, we said, has given three major answers to what the soul wants—Existentialist, Freudian, Jungian—depending upon how the word *want* was understood, as a dreadful abyss, as a wish for fulfilment, as a

want
(desire)

E = dreadful abyss
F = wish for fulfilment
J = seeking of wholeness

seeking for wholeness. We can read from Adler yet another: the soul's want is the soul's lack, what fails it as *wo es fehlt*. This answer says that inferiority is basic to it and is not only the effect of the spirit's fantasy of perfection. The ground of its want are the *inferiores*, the deepest psychic figures of the underworld whose voices void all positive assurance by breaking down, making small, and keeping low the substantiations that neglect inferiority. The soul's want is given with it, like the want of Aristophanes' her-maphrodite in the *Symposium*, like the want of the souls in Hades, and the wants of the voices in the dialogues we heard.

Does not this want of the soul reflect the essential nature of Eros whose mother was Penia (poverty, neediness, want)? And is it not this want which is present each time we are in love, whether in the transference of therapy or in the love that develops while engaged with a piece of imaginative work, a poem or novel? Even as we are inventive and resourceful (Eros' father was Poros, clever resourcefulness),[24] we are nonetheless at a loss. Eros itself brings us to inferiortiy, to that consternation that we are not enough, have not the ability, that our very soul is wanting and so is ever in want. Need is the mother of the soul's erotic plight; the soul's want is inescapably linked to its eros, that which it seems to want most and yet which is also the origin of that want.

If the soul's want is *a priori*, then loss is a permanent possibility of soul. We may most have soul or be in soul (*esse in anima*) when we sense most its loss. Then the sense of want belongs to the ontology of soul and to what we mean by 'being psychological.' No psychological act can fully satisfy, no interpretation truly click like a key in a lock, no relationship of souls complete the lack and failure that reflects the essence of psyche. Imperfection is in its essence, and we are complete only by being in want. There will always be a mistake which is precisely what gives value to psychotherapeutic courage. Psychotherapy can only stay with its own inferiority if it is to remain psychotherapeutic.

But, like the patients in the dialogues, psychotherapy has difficulty hearing the voices of its own *inferiores*. It too would move away from its shadows, its sickness, its ancestors. This move away from inferiority is "psychotherapy's inferiority complex," which appears in the practice of the hour and the remembrance of its history which have been built not on positive knowledge but in response to souls in want; and even this psychotherapeutic response is as many-sided and self-contradictory as its founders. Part of this history is Alfred Adler, the 'lesser' member of the ancestors. Our recovery of Adler in this chapter has been intended to restore him to us and with him his contribution to psychotherapy's inferiority.

For the whole therapeutic opus with its vision of perfection in the love of fellow-feeling can never leave the tiny beginning, the bit of gravel in the shoe, the *petite tache humide* that returns us to feelings of inferiority which are given with embodiment in our organic creatureliness. And so, even our answers to "What does the soul want?" do not put us on top of the question. We are not coming out all right; *all* shall not be well. We are, however, attempting to remain in touch with the soul by means of the question. For psychotherapy it may be enough to remember—not *what* it wants—but *that* it wants, and that the soul's eternal wanting is psychotherapy's eternal question.

References and Abbreviations

NC   Adler, Alfred. *The Neurotic Constitution*. Translated by B. Glueck and J.E. Lind. New York: Moffat Yard, 1917.

OI   _____ . *Study of Organ Inferiority and Its Psychical Compensation: A Contribution to Clinical Medicine*. Translated by S.E. Jelliffe. New York: Nervous and Mental Disease Publ. Co., 1917. Johnson Reprint, 1970.

U   _____ . *Understanding Human Nature*. Translated by W.B. Wolfe. London: Allen & Unwin, 1928.

IP   _____ . *The Practice and Theory of Individual Psychology*. Translated by Paul Radin. London: Routledge, 1929.

L   _____ . *What Life Should Mean to You*. London: Unwin Books, 1932, 1962.

Lou   Andreas-Salome, Lou. *The Freud Journal of Lou Andreas-Salome*. Translated by Stanley A. Leavy. London: Hogarth, 1965.

A&A   Ansbacher, Heinz L., and Ansbacher, Rowena R. *The Individual Psychology of Alfred Adler*. New York: Harper Torchbook, 1964.

El   Ellenberger, Henri F. *The Discovery of the Unconscious*. London: Allen Lane, Penguin Press, 1970.

CW   Jung, C.W. *Collected Works of C.G. Jung*, Bollingen Series. Translated by R.C.F. Hull. Princeton: Princeton Univ. Press.

FJL   McGuire, Wm., ed. *The Freud/Jung Letters*. Bollingen Series. Princeton: Princeton Univ. Press, 1974.

O'C '67   O'Connell, Walter E. "Individual Psychology." *New Catholic Encyclopedia*, 1967.

O'C '76   _____ . "The 'Friends of Adler' Phenomenon." *J. Indiv. Psychol.* 32/1 (1976).

O'C '77   _____ . "The Sense of Humor: Actualizer of Persons and Theories." In *It's a Funny Thing, Humour*, edited by A. Chapman and H. Foot. Oxford: Pergamon, 1977.

Spr   *Spring: An Annual of Archetypal Psychology and Jungian Thought*. New York/Zurich: Spring Publications, 1970-1983.

V   Vaihinger, Hans. *The Philosophy of 'As If.' "* 2nd ed. Translated by C.K. Ogden. London: Routledge, 1935.

W   Way, Lewis. *Alfred Adler, An Introduction to his Psychology*. Harmondsworth: Penguin, 1956.

Notes

Notes

1. The Fiction of Case History

1. Giovanni Papini (1881-1956), Italian pragmatist philosopher and writer. Cf. *The Encyclopedia of Philosophy* (New York: Macmillan, 1967) vol. 6. *See* "Papini."

2. G. Papini, "A Visit to Freud," reprinted in *Review of Existential Psychology and Psychiatry 9*, n. 2 (1969): 130-34.

3. J. Hillman, *Re-Visioning Psychology* (New York: Harper & Row, 1975).

4. S. Freud, *Collected Papers III*, "Case Histories," trans. A. and J. Strachey, 3rd ed. (London: Hogarth, 1946). For some recent discussions of Freud's cases as literature, *see* S. Marcus, "Freud und Dora. Roman, Geschichte, Krankengeschichte," *Psyche* 1974 (28), pp. 32-79; L. Freeman, "Bibliography" in her *The Story of Anna O.* (New York: Walker, 1972). Since D. H. Thomas' *The White Hotel*, there are many more.

5. Roger Fowler, ed., *A Dictionary of Modern Critical Terms* (London and Boston: Routledge & Kegan Paul, 1973). *See* "technique."

6. E. M. Forster, *Aspects of the Novel* (1927; reprint ed., Harmondsworth: Penguin, 1962), pp. 37-38.

7. I have heard that the last work Freud read as he was dying was Balzac's *Peau de chagrin*.

8. Quoted by Forster, *Aspects*, p. 54.

9. Freud, *Collected Papers III*, p. 24. Freud's defense of the patient's defenses (timidity and shame) also provides him the occasion to intervene as narrator between the story and the reader. This device is fundamental to storytelling: "In imaginative literature the nature of the link between the reader and the text is crucial, and here the *narrator* becomes important. Narrative has two overlapping aspects. One is a question of content, the assemblage of material; the other is rhetorical, how the narrative is presented to the audience." Fowler, *Critical Terms*. *See* "narrative."

10. Cf. my "Methodological Problems in Dream Research" in my *Loose Ends—Primary Papers in Archetypal Psychology* (New York/Zürich: Spring Publications, 1975), pp. 196-98.

11. Also in *Collected Papers III*. The best discussion and bibliography of the Schreber case is that by Roberto Calasso appended to the Italian translation of Schreber's *Memoirs* (Milano: Adelphi, 1974).

12. Quoted by Forster, *Aspects*, p. 54, from Alain's *Système des beaux arts* (Paris: 1920, pp. 314-15).

13. Forster, *Aspects*, pp. 93-95.

14. Fowler, *Critical Terms. See* "plot."

15. First definition of history from J. M. Baldwin, *Dictionary of Philosophy and Psychology* (New York: Macmillan, 1925). *See* "history."

16. A. J. Ayer, *The Foundations of Empirical Knowledge* (London: Macmillan, 1969), p. 79.

17. Hans Vaihinger, *The Philosophy of 'As If'*, trans. C. K. Ogden (London: Routledge & Kegan Paul, 1935); cf. the relevance of as-if fictions for archetypal psychology in my *Re-Visioning Psychology*, pp. 153ff.

18. One who has explored fictional modes for the *vision* an analyst has toward a case is Roy Schafer, "The Psychoanalytic Vision of Reality," *International Journal Psycho-Analysis* 51 (1970): 279-97, 1970. Schafer finds four basic visions in psychoanalytic writing: comic, romantic, tragic, and ironic (acknowledging his debt to Northrop Frye who in turn acknowledges his to Jung).

19. Wolfgang Giegerich, "Ontogeny = Phylogeny?" *Spring 1975* (New York/Zürich: Spring Publ.), p. 118.

20. My "On Senex Consciousness," *Spring 1970* (New York/Zürich: Spring Publications), 146-65. Also on Saturn from the psychological viewpoint, A. Vitale, "Saturn: The Transformation of the Father," in *Fathers and Mothers: Essays by Five Hands* (New York/Zürich: Spring Publications) pp. 5-39.

21. Patricia Berry, "An Approach to the Dream," in her *Echo's Subtle Body* (Dallas: Spring Publ., 1982).

22. Fowler, *Critical Terms. See* "hero."

23. On Saturn and reduction, see P. Berry, "On Reduction," *op. cit.* and my "The 'Negative' Senex and a Renaissance Solution," *Spring 1975* (New York/Zürich: Spring Publ.), pp. 88ff.

24. Annabel M. Patterson, *Hermogenes and the Renaissance: Seven Ideas of Style* (Princeton: Princeton Univ. Press, 1970).

25. J. Hillman, *Suicide and the Soul* [1964] (Dallas: Spring Publ., 1978), pp. 77-79.

26. All references to Jung unless otherwise indicated are to *The Collected Works of C.G. Jung* (Bollingen Series 20) translated by R. F. C. Hull and edited by H. Read, M. Fordham, G. Adler, and W. McGuire (Princeton: Princeton Univ. Press), hereinafter *CW* with volume number and paragraph.

27. *CW* 8, §§477, 809, 451, 843, 457, 303; *CW* 7, §§44, 75, 206; *CW* 16, §§91, 307, 335, 464; *CW* 10, §§29, 627.

28. H. H. Walser. "An Early Psychoanalytical Tragedy," *Spring 1974* (New York/Zürich: Spring Publ.), p. 248n.

29. On the relation between Jung's ideas and his case history, see A. Jaffé "The Creative Phases in Jung's Life," *Spring 1972* (New York/Zürich: Spring Publ.), pp. 162-90.

30. *CW* 10, §1042. Cf. *CW* 9, §319f. for further reason why Jung does not go into case history in the usual sense.

31. On Jung and Hermes, see D. C. Noel, "Veiled Kabir: C. G. Jung's Phallic Self-Image," *Spring 1974* (New York/Zürich: Spring Publ.), esp. pp. 235-40.

32. Gay Clifford, *Transformations of Allegory* (London: Routledge, 1974).

33. Fowler, *Critical Terms. See* "allegory."

34. On the history of the Dionysos/Apollo contrast, see J. Ritter, ed. *Historisches Wörterbuch der Philosophie* (Basel/Stuttgart: Schwabe 1971), "Apollonische/dionysische," vol. 1, p. 422. On Jung's ideas of Dionysos see my "Dionysus in Jung's Writings," *Spring 1972;* on the Apollo-Dionysos contrast my *The Myth of Analysis*, part 3 (Evanston: Northwestern, 1972); Gerald Holton, "On Being Caught between Dionysians and Apollonians," *Daedalus*, Summer 1974, pp. 65-81; on the Greek god himself the indispensable works are W. F. Otto, *Dionysus*, trans. R. B. Palmer (New York/Züich: Spring Publ., 1981),

and K. Kerényi, *Dionysus*, trans. R. Manheim (Princeton: Princeton Univ. Press, 1976). Modern works on the theme are often misleading because they do not give a full enough picture of either Dionysos or Apollo, and this because they are themselves caught by these Gods in their polarity and thus they express archetypal-stereotypical views. For instance, P. E. Slater, *The Glory of Hera* (Boston: Beacon, 1968), M. K. Spears, *Dionysus and the City* (New York: Oxford Univ. Press, 1970). As I pointed out in my paper on Jung's Dionysos, our general image of this God is Nietzschean, Wotanic, Germanic. For a collection of material on this Germanic Dionysos, see: J. H. W. Rosteutscher, *Die Wiederkunft des Dionysos* (Bern: Francke Verlag, 1947).

35. *Hamlet*, II, 2.
36. The classical difference between memory and imagination is only that 'remembered' images have the quality of time added. This distinction comes from Aristotle, cf. Frances Yates, *The Art of Memory* (London: Routledge & Kegan Paul, 1966), p. 32ff.
37. When Sallust explains the nature of myths, he writes "All this did not happen at any one time but always is so." Sallustius, *Concerning the Gods and the Universe*, IV, Ed. Arthur Darby Nock, (Cambridge Univ. Press, 1926).
38. Cf. K. R. Popper, *The Poverty of Historicism* (London: Routledge & Kegan Paul, 1969). Popper takes the first step into a discussion of history as a psychological need. But he is speaking of a particular view and use of history: historicism. We are opening the question further: why the historical mode at all?
39. Peter Burke, *The Renaissance Sense of the Past* (London: Arnold, 1969), p. 105.
40. E. S. Casey, "Toward a Phenomenology of Imagination," *J. British Society Phenomenology 5* (1974), p. 10.
41. I have discussed at length the relation between imagination and childhood in my "Abandoning the Child," *Eranos 40—1971*.
42. Differences in case-history writing follow old conventions. Social realism's interest in craven and trivial detail requires the low style or writing of things of everyday life. The Jungian style is 'high' with its archetypal resonances to heroic, tribal, and mythic events; it follows the Classical and Renaissance idea of history which "excluded 'low' people, things, or words" (Burke, ibid.).
43. The term "soul-making," and the idea of its taking place in the "vale of the world," is from John Keats, see my discussions in *The Myth of Analysis* and *Re-Visioning Psychology*.
44. For an excellent presentation of soul-making and psychotherapy through words, *see* Pedro Lain Entralgo, *The Therapy of the Word in Classical Antiquity*, trans. L. J. Rather and J. M. Sharp (New Haven: Yale Univ. Press, 1970).

2. The Pandaemonium of Images

1. C. G. Jung/A. Jaffé, *Memories, Dreams, Reflections,* transl. R. & C. Winston (N. Y.: Pantheon, 1961).

2. S. Leavy, "A Footnote to Jung's 'Memories,' " *Psychoanalytic Q.* 33, 1964, pp. 567-574.

3. C. G. Jung, *Collected Works (CW)* 7, § 183, transl. R. F. C. Hull (Princeton: Princeton Univ. Press and London: Routledge). Further on the daimon as allotter of fate, B. C. Dietrich, *Death, Fate and the Gods* (London: Athlone, 1967), pp. 18, 57.

4 Cf. R. Grinnell, "Reflections on the Archetype of Consciousness—Personality and Psychological Faith," *Spring 1970,* Spring Publ., 1970, pp. 30-39.

5. Jung/Jaffé, *Memories,* p. 181.

6. *Idem,* pp. 182-183.

7. Cf. Mt. 24: 4 & 24 (though daimons are not directly mentioned), 8: 31, 9: 32, 11: 18, 15: 22; similarly Mk. 1: 32, 5: 12; Js. 3: 15, 2: 19. Other NT statements on daimons are referred to in footnotes below.

8. For an introduction to the literature on daimons and demonology see *RGG* "Dämonen; " van der Leeuw, *Religion in Essence and Manifestation* I: 14, 15, 40, 42 (on daimons, angels, plural souls, external souls); Rohde, *Psyche.* For more modern works see: F. A. Wilford, "Daimon in Homer," *Numen XII/3, 1965, pp. 217-232;* R. H. Barrow, *Plutarch and his Times* (Bloomington/London: Indiana Univ. Press, 1969), pp. 86-91 and G. Soury, *La démonologie de Plutarque* (Paris, 1942); on the subject in antiquity as a whole, M. Detienne, *La Notion de "daimon" dans le pythagorisme ancien* (Paris, Belles Lettres, 1963); E. R. Dodds, "Man and the Daemonic World" in his *Pagan and Christian in an Age of Anxiety* (Cambridge: University Press, 1965); A. Cook, "Daimon" in his *Enactment: Greek Tragedy* (Chicago: Swallow Press, 1971). Particularly insightful passages can be found in: R. B. Onians, *The Origins of European Thought* (Cambridge: University Press, 1953), v. index; D. O'Brien, *Empedocles' Cosmic Cycle* (Cambridge: University Press, 1969), pp. 85-97, 325-336; A. D. Nock, "The Emperor's Divine Comes," *Essays on Religion and the Ancient World* (Oxford: Clarendon, 1972), pp. 664 ff; D. P. Walker, *Spiritual and Demonic Magic from Ficino to Campanella* (Univ. Notre Dame Press, 1975), pp. 42-55 & passim; E. R. Dodds, "Commentary" to *Proclus' The Elements of Theology* (Oxford: University Press, 1963), pp. 249 ff. Also of value; E. Benz, *Die Vision—Erfahrungsformen und Bilderwelt* (Stuttgart: Klett, 1969); O. Diethelm, "The Medical Teaching of Demonology in the 17th and 18th Centuries," *J. Hist. Behav. Science* VI/1, 1970, pp. 3-15; R. May, "Psychotherapy and the Daimonic" in J. Campbell, ed., *Myths, Dreams, and Religion* N. Y.: Dutton, 1970), pp. 196-210; P. Friedländer, "Demon and Eros" Vol. 1, Chap. 2 of his *Plato,* transl. H. Meyerhoff (N. Y.: Pantheon, 1958). "Excursus on the History of the Doctrine of Daemons" in J. A. Stewart, *The Myths of Plato* (London: Centaur Press), 1960, pp. 384-401.

9. For the Homeric Greek, "one's identity is largely couched in terms of the *story,* or *stories* of one's life. The events in which a man participated... constitute his identity. If the version of the events is different, then the identity is different." B. Simon & H. Weiner, "Models of Mind and Mental Illness in Ancient Greece, I," *J. Hist. Behav. Science* II, 1966,

p. 308. Since Gods participate in these stories, they are myths, and one's biography becomes one's mythology. Self-knowledge or 'introspection' is in later Greek thought an "examining, sorting out, and scrutinizing" of these "stories."

10. E. Gendlin, "Focusing," *Psychotherapy* 6/1, 1969, pp. 4-15. This excellent paper is paradigmatic for showing the limitations of introspection in phenomenological and body-referent therapies. Self-examination never leaves the 'inside' of its own consciousness.

11. R. Poole, *Towards Deep Subjectivity* (London: Allen Lane, Penguin, 1972). Here the depth dimension never truly descends below the historical ego and its feelings. The appeal to a "totality of multiple perspectives" remains an egocentric humanism, without the divine cosmoi that link the various perspectives through myths and that provide their root metaphors and their communities of meanings in which they are necessary. In the absence of archetypal persons who provide truly deep (in the sense of beyond) subjectivities that are not my own, existential and phenomenological humanism remains blind to its own infrastructures. It becomes a secular radical relativism, or solipsism of contesting personal feelings (which Poole admits), a mere way of opinion which does not change by increasing the quantity of opinions. While championing multiple subjective perspectives, this position betrays impiety toward their source. For, by putting all the eyes in the head of omniscient man (a totality of viewpoints), or in an introjection of committee man, the Gods who are actually using our eyes are ignored. It is the Gods alone who make radical relativism legitimate, and tolerable. But once they have been admitted we have left Poole (who speaks for Protagoras, Husserl, Sartre, Laing, Kierkegaard, etc. and their humanism) for the imagistic precision of an archetypal psychology. Then deep subjectivity refers to the *subjects* in my depths.

12. *CW* 8: §§ 204, 627, 712; *CW* 6, §§ 174f (based on Schiller), 383; also "Comments on a Passage from Nietzsche's *Zarathustra*" *Spring 1972*, pp. 152-154. These paragraphs are illustrative of Jung's *religious* conception of the complex.

13. Cf. J. Kamerbeek, "Dilthey versus Nietzsche," *Studia Philos.* X, 1950, pp. 52ff for a collection of passages in which both authors attack introspection.

14. F. Nietzsche, *Human, All-Too-Human* II, Maxim 223, transl. O. Levy (Edinburgh: Foulis).

15. Jung/Jaffé, *Memories*, pp. 192-193.

16. Compare Jaspers below for a similar reaction, in terms of morality, as soon as he begins to discuss daimons. For a profound inquiry into the moral question in relation to archetypal images, see R. Grinnell, "In Praise of the 'Instinct for Unholiness'—Intimations of a Moral Archetype," *Spring 1971*, pp. 168-185.

17. Jung/Jaffé, *Memories*, p. 183.

18. *Idem*, p. 319.

19. On the distinction and relation between soul and spirit, see my *Re-Visioning Psychology* (N.Y.: Harper & Row, 1975), pp. 67-70; also my "Anima II," *Spring 1974* (N.Y./Zurich: Spring Publ.), pp. 144-145.

20. K. Jaspers, *The Perennial Scope of Philosophy*, R. Manheim, transl. (London: Routledge,

1950), p. 177. Jaspers had earlier examined and condemned "the mythological-daemonic Weltbild" particularly as exemplified in Goethe, in K. Jaspers, *Psychologie der Weltanschaung* (Berlin: Springer, 1919), pp. 166-172.

21. K. Barth, *Die kirchliche Dogmatik*, III, 3, p. 608f.

22. Quoted from D.P. Gray, *The One and the Many: Teilhard de Chardin's Vision of Unity* (London: Burns & Oates, 1969), p. 21. Cf. my *The Myth of Analysis*, part one (N.Y.: Harper & Row, 1978), for a variety of archetypal notions of creativity. Teilhard's view here is clearly the perspective of the senex archetype.

23. Cf. *CW* 8, § 388ff, "The Unconscious as a Multiple Consciousness," and § 582.

24. The problem is already put in Mark 1:34 where it is stated that Jesus "suffered not the devils to speak."

25. W. Theiler, "Die Sprache des Geistes in der Antike," *Forschungen zum Neuplatonismus* (Berlin, 1966), pp. 302-312.

26. Differences between spirit language and soul language can be found in my "Peaks and Vales," in *Puer Papers*, Spring Publ., 1979.

27. "Reality consists of a multiplicity of things. But one is not a number; the first number is two, and with it multiplicity and reality begin." *CW* 14, § 659; also the passage on multiplicity in his *Septem Sermones ad Mortuos*, IV: "The multiplicity of the Gods corres-pondeth to the multiplicity of man." "The unity of consciousness or of the so-called personality is not a reality at all but a desideratum" (*CW* 9, i, § 190).

28. Cf. Jung/Jaffé, *Memories*, pp. 185-188; *CW* 8, §§ 172-179.

29. Compare Jaspers' radical dualism ("nothing in between") with this passage from Plato (Diotima speaking in the *Symposium*): "Everything that is daimonic is intermediate between God and mortal. Interpreting and conveying the wishes of men to Gods and the will of Gods to men, it stands between the two and fills the gap... God has no contact with man; only through the daimonic is there intercourse and conversation between men and Gods, whether in the waking state or during sleep. And the man who is expert in such intercourse is a daimonic man...." (Dodds transl., *Pagan and Christian*, p. 37). Plutarch carried this further, saying that he who denies the daimons breaks the chain that unites the world to God (*De defectu Orac.* 13). Clearly, as C. Bigg points out in *The Christian Platonists of Alexandria*, (Oxford: Clarendon, 1913, 1968, pp. 307-308): "The doctrine of the Daemons properly understood would... make the belief in Christ unnecessary." Thus the issue concerns the nature of the mediator—either the one historical person, Christ and the Cross (axis mundi), or the plural imaginal persons. Hence the sign of the cross as protection against daimons. The same use may be made of the 'psychological cross,' i.e., the mandala which arose in Jung's mind in the same period as his meeting with the daimons and which, in his writings on the mandala, is presented as a refuge against the incursions of psychic powers (*CW* 9, 1, §§ 16, 710). (On the Cross in relation with the multiple powers, see *CW* 11, § 429.) As Jung further shows, the collapse of this *axis mundi* (Christianity as mediator) resurrects the daimons—and in their former higher place, "as things seen in the skies" (UFO's, *CW* 10, § 635), with the same descriptive terms employed by Iamblichus for daimons (see below):

rapidity, luminosity, etc. The official religion of today (science, military, government) through its bureaus of *inspectio* has declared these daimons, too, 'non-existent,' whereas folk belief continues to 'see' them and bring witness.

30. That the soul as mediator is also that which keeps distinctions is Iamblichus' elaboration of the logic of the third realm in his Law of Mean Terms: "Two dissimilar terms must be linked by an intermediary having something in common with each of them." Thus the soul mediates because it has something in common with both the world and the divine, at the same time "keeping them firmly apart." Quotations and discussion from R.T. Wallis, *Neo-Platonism* (London: Duckworth, 1972), p. 131.

31. Cf. my note on this Proteus image in Jung and in the Renaissance, *Re-Visioning Psychology*, p. 256, n. 73.

32. That the daimons teach us the as-if thinking of myth was already noted by Proclus ("An Apology for the Fables of Homer," *Thomas Taylor the Platonist: Selected Writings*, K. Raine and G.M. Harper, eds. (Princeton: Univ. Press, 1969), p. 461: ". . . we may especially perceive the alliance of these fables with the tribe of daemons, whose energies manifest many things symbolically, as those know who have met with daemons when awake, or have enjoyed their inspiration in dreams. . . ."

33. H. Stierlin, "Karl Jaspers' Psychiatry in the Light of his Basic Philosophical Position," *J. Hist. Behav. Science* X, 2, 1974, p. 221. Stierlin's charge that Jaspers failed with schizophrenia is another way of stating that he failed with daimons.

34. *CW* 5, § 388.

35. F.A. Yates, *The Art of Memory* (London: Routledge, 1966), p. 10.

36. The Iconoclast Controversy is thoroughly reviewed by C.J. Hefele *A History of the Councils of the Church*, transl. W.R. Clark (Edinburgh: Clark, 1896), V: 260-301. See also some relevant documents in English by Cyril Mango, *The Art of the Byzantine Empire 312-1453*, (Englewood Cliffs: Prentice Hall, 1972), pp. 149-177.

37. Eusebius, *Hist. eccl.* vii 18, cf. I.P. Sheldon-Williams, "The Philosophy of Icons," in *Cambridge History of Later Greek and Early Medieval Philosophy*, A.H. Armstrong ed. (Cambridge Univ. Press, 1970), p. 515.

38. Hefele, pp. 378-385.

39. Hefele, pp. 371-372 (Report on the Fifth Session of the Council.) Cf. Leonide Ouspensky, *Theology of the Ikon*, (Crestwood N.Y.: St. Vladimir's Seminary Press, 1978), pp. 145-178. ". . . the council specifies and particularly emphasizes that our attitude towards the image should be one of respect and veneration, but not one of true adoration, which belongs only to God. . ." (p. 170). The council's Greek term for this veneration was *proskunesis*. This word has connotations of greeting, welcoming, even kissing, which suggests that the relation with the images is via anima.

40. On the one hand, the iconophils held, in the words of John Damascene, III (*v. inf.* note. 43): "An image is a likeness and a representation of some one, *containing in itself the person who is imaged*." (ital. mine.) On the other hand, the official position, as further clarified in the Council of 869-870 (Hefele, *Conciliengeschichte* IV, § 402, Canon 3): "The holy image of Our Lord Jesus Christ, like the Books of the Evangelists, shall be venerated; for

just as the words of writings lead us to salvation, so do images work through colors, and all, learned and unlearned, *find them useful*" (transl. & ital. mine). The doctrinal decision further states: "For each time that we see their representation in an image, each time, while gazing upon them, we are made to remember the prototypes. . . ." Ouspensky, *op. cit.*, p. 160. The images are means of mediating with the prototypes—a view which always implies images are of a second, lesser order of being.

41. Jung (*CW* 8, § 92) connects the "extermination of polytheism" with the Christian suppression of "individual symbol-formation." "But as the intensity of the Christian idea begins to fade, a recrudescence of individual symbol-formation may be expected." This does not disallow the symbol-formation from being Christian, as it was in Jung's own case.

42. Sheldon-Williams, *op. cit.*, p. 512.

43. John Damascene, *On Holy Images*, Mary H. Allies, transl. (London: Thos. Baker, 1898).

44. St. Basil, *De Spiritu Sancto* XVIII, in Sheldon-Williams, p. 509.

45. The fact is generally overlooked that Otto transposed a Roman term from the imagistic context of polytheism into a Judeo-Christian theological feeling. *The Idea of the Holy (Das Heilige)* is said to have had its source in an experience of the "numinous" in a Tangier Synagogue. (R. Schinzer, "Rudolf Otto—Entwurf einer Biographie," in E. Benz, ed., *Rudolf Otto's Bedeutung für die Religionswissenschaft und die Theologie heute* (Leiden: Brill, 1971), p. 17; idem (in more detail), p. 37 in Benz's article. Otto's experience and Lutheran language continue to affect Jungian psychology (e.g., when the Self and other archetypes are supposedly recognized particularly through 'numinous' events) without cognizance that a *numen* is an image. 'Numinous,' therefore, implies not a wholly other Holy Power, but rather the religious nature of an *image*.

46. *CW* 13, § 75; on complex as "image" *CW* 8, § 201 and as "person" § 202.

47. *CW* 11, § 889.

48. *CW* 14, § 753.

49. *The Collected Poems of Wallace Stevens* (London: Faber, 1955), p. 463: "The Study of Images I."

50. *CW* 6, § 743.

51. *The Collected Poems of Wallace Stevens*, p. 440: "A Primitive Like an Orb."

52. *CW* 6, § 78.

53. The problem of moral dualism in regard to daimons (Jaspers' division into "benevolent and malignant") is supposedly—as so many Western dualisms are said to be—a Persian influence which radically separates the forces of good (angels) who are with God from the forces of Ahriman (evil daimons). Yet, as A.D. Nock says, "The terms [*theoi* & *daimones*] do not in general involve any antithesis as of good and evil." "Greeks and Magi," *Essays*, Vol. II: 520. Dodds (*Pagan and Christian*, p. 118n) finds the dualism native to Plutarch who refers to Empedocles. (Cf. Plutarch's *De Iside et Osiride*, Transl. & Comm. J.W. Griffiths [Univ. Wales Press, 1970], pp. 24-28, 383f.) But is it not Paul who brought the issue of dualism in regard to daimons to an impossible head in I Cor. 10: 19-21? Immediately after condemning images, he says: "Ye cannot drink the cup of the

Lord, and the cup of demons." Either/Or. Neoplatonism tried to resolve the dualism with pluralism, by stringing them out on a differentiated vertical chain through the middle region. Jung's differentiation of the psyche by means of personified figures (shadow, child, mother, senex, anima/us, etc.) compares with the Neoplatonic efforts. Both structure the soul in terms of kinds of imaginal persons. So, too, Guilio Camillo's Theatre in the Art of Memory. These are each demonologies, which turn to a plurality of personified mythical divinities (archetypes) for their organization of the soul, and which place the organizing factors in the soul itself, the imagination.

54. Wallis, Neo-Platonism, p. 109.
55. Iamblichus, On the Mysteries of the Egyptians, Chaldeans, and Assyrians, transl. T. Taylor (1821) (London: Watkins, 1968), II, § 3.
56. Ibid. I, § 20. (The questions put by Porphyry in an Epistle to Anebo are translated in the same volume, pp. 1-16.)
57. Cf. Wallis, Neo-Platonism, p. 152 for a diagram of the hierarchy.
58. Cf. Dietrich, "The Daemon and the Hero," Chap. II, Death, Fate and the Gods, for a comprehensive discussion.
59. The spirit/soul distinction is basic to Jung's work from a paper on this problem in 1919 (CW 8, §§ 570ff.) to the grand opus on their conjunction (CW 14). See also n. 19 sup.
60. Iamblichus, op. cit., p. 260 (a note by T. Taylor quoting Proclus' First Alcibiades commentary).
61. The daimonic mode presents itself not only in images. It appears also in reflection, or as Nock says: "It must be remembered that, as Wilamowitz and Nilsson have taught us, the word daimon is extremely rare in cult. It is a word of reflection and analysis." ("The Cult of Heroes," Essays II: 580n.) The daimonic mode appears in our mythologizings about an event after an event. This was implied above n. 32, where Proclus allies the "tribe of daemons" with the mythical manner of telling.
62. In the 10th session, 11th Canon, of the Church Council of 869, man was officially dichotomized into a material and immaterial duality. The immaterial part merged soul with spirit. An essential distinction was lost. The elimination of soul had already been prepared in the Council of 789 (see above) with the taming of images. The lesson is clear; history recapitulates in psychology. Once the image is deprived of its autonomy and power, there is no longer experiential evidence for 'soul' which then declines, without the image, into a mere (theological) concept without necessity.
63. The Collected Poems of Wallace Stevens, p. 463: "The Study of Images I."
64. Cf. R. F. C. Hull, "Bibliographical Notes on Active Imagination in the Works of C. G. Jung," Spring 1971 (Zurich/N.Y.: Spring Publ., 1971), pp. 115-120, for a full list of passages.
65. CW 14, § 707 ff. (Part VI, 6 "Self-Knowledge").
66. CW 14, §§ 708, 749.
67. Jung emphasizes holding "an Internal Talk of one person with another who is invisible, as in the invocation of the Deity, or communion with one's self, or with one's good angel" (quotation from Ruland's alchemical dictionary, CW 14, § 707).

68. Jung's quotation of Freud's warning to him, Jung/Jaffé, *Memories*, p. 150.
69. Popularist superstitious theurgy (working upon the Gods) is always attributed to Neoplatonism and about this there is much hot debate, e. g., A. A. Barb, "The Survival of the Magic Arts" in A. Momigliano, ed., *The Conflict between Paganism and Christianity in the Fourth Century*, (Oxford: Clarendon, 1963). Indeed, a 'higher' theurgy (or white magic) was recommended by Iamblichus. One root of the popularism in Neoplatonism (or Jungian active imagination) is its psychological style of thought, thinking in 'invisibles.' Thus, theurgy was recommended by some Neoplatonists (Iamblichus, *Mysteries*, V, 15-17) in order to bring 'body' into the philosophy; or (for Porphyry) theurgy is an easy introduction for simple and vulgar minds (i. e., the mind that works literalistically and in the concrete only) for communicating with the Powers. But fundamentally, as Plotinus insisted (*Enn.* II, 9, 14), theurgy cannot aid the soul's return to the Intelligible order. At best, such theurgy (guided imagery) is a counter-magic for immediate practical effects (*Enn.* IV, 4, 43) or what psychotherapy now calls a 'counter-phobic ritual.' See discussion and references in: Wallis, *Neo-Platonism*, pp. 71; & 3, 14, 108f., 153; Dodd's (1947) "Theurgy," Appendix II in his *The Greeks and the Irrational* (Boston, Beacon, 1957); D. P. Walker, *Spiritual and Demonic Magic, op. cit.*
70. Porphyry's *Life of Plotinus*, 10, 33-38, from Wallis, p. 71.
71. That self-knowledge is endless is not only Heraclitean (the soul is without end) and Socratic (self-knowledge is ultimately the study of dying, as well as of the Divine—*First Alcibiades* 127d ff., also where *self* is interpreted as *soul*), it is also Judeo-Islamic, where Know Thyself means, fundamentally, Knowledge of God (*Homo imago Dei*): "He who knows himself knows his Lord." Cf. A. Altmann, "The Delphic Maxim in Medieval Islam and Judaism" in his *Studies in Religious Philosophy and Mysticism*, (London: Routledge, 1969), pp. 1-40 with rich notes. In keeping with this tradition I have in this paper consistently understood the Delphic 'self' as 'soul,' *nefesh, nafs, nafashu, psyché, anima.*
72. Jung's discussion in the last part of the *Mysterium Coniunctionis* concerning self-knowledge and active imagination returns continually to Mercurius who seems thus to be both the secret (hermetic) 'knower' and object of the knowing, *CW* 14, §§ 705 to end.
73. "Multiplication . . . consists in recommencing the operation that has already been performed, but with exalted and perfected matters, and not with crude substances . . . The whole secret . . . is a physical dissolution in Mercury . . ." M. Ruland, *A Lexicon of Alchemy* (1612), transl. A. E. Waite (London: Watkins, 1964). The implication is clear: the operation requires dissolving the physicality of an impulse (a 'projection' as the alchemists also called it) again in the psychological (Mercury); and, rather than operating in the terms of today's crude substantialities, i. e., behavioral sociological materialisms, recommencing the psychological work but now with further subtlety.
74. Again the figure is Mercurius *multi flores* "who tempts us into a world of sense" and whose habitation is in the veins swollen with blood (*CW* 13, § 209). A basic alchemical maxim says that the work is spoiled if "the reddening comes too soon," in this case, if the work enters the world before having stained the soul.

3. What Does the Soul Want

1. His questions attempt to divide the psychic hermaphrodite; see below, *Neurotic Thinking and the Hermaphrodite.*

2. For the astrologically-minded, the triumvirate were each born in fixed signs (Freud: May 6, *Taurus*; Adler: February 7, *Aquarius*; Jung: July 28, *Leo*) and their agreement is more surprising than their intolerance and holding of their own positions.

3. A recent comparative sketch has been made by R. J. Huber and R. Steir, "Social Interest and Individuation: A Comparison of Jung and Adler," *Charac. Potential*, 7, 1976, pp. 174-180. Standard works of comparison were done in middle years of this century ('comparative schools of depth psychology') two of which were introduced by Jung: G. Adler (*Entdeckung der Seele*, 1934) and W. M. Kranefeldt (*Secret Ways of the Mind*, 1930, '32, '34).

4. J. Thompson Rowling, "Pathological Changes in Mummies," *Proc. Roy. Soc. Med.* 54, 1961, p. 410. Erik Hornung informs me that the correlation between organ and divinity was not at all strict; we dare not read the freedom of Egyptian polytheistic fantasy with the systematic identities of our monotheistic mentality.

5. On the relation of psychic image and body organ in Jungian thought, see Jung, "Psychological Commentary on Kundalini Yoga," *Spring 1976 & 1977*; G. R. Heyer, *The Organism of the Mind* (trans. E. & C. Paul), (London: Kegan Paul, 1933); S. R. Bach, *Spontaneous Paintings of Severely Ill Patients*, (Documenta Geigy, Acta Psychosomatica, Basel, 1966), 1969.

6. The 'dialectic nature of reality' proposed by psychologists from Heraclitus through Coleridge to Jung and philosophers such as Hegel and Marx, as well as the 'dialectic method' (Nietzsche, for instance) can be severely taken to task from an Adlerian perspective as neurotic modes of thinking, if these modes are not seen as pragmatic instruments or hypothetical fictions, having in their background the mastery of variety. See further: R. H. Dolliver, "Alfred Adler and the Dialectic," *J. Hist. Behav. Sci.* X/1, 1974, pp. 16-20; H. L. Ansbacher, Chap. 3 "Masculine Protest: A Term of Cultural Psychology" typescript of a forthcoming work (courtesy of the author, 1977).

7. "Der Psychische Hermaphroditismus im Leben und in der Neurose," *Fortschritte d. Medizin*, 28, 1910, 486-493, and discussed most recently by Ansbacher, "Chap 3," typescript, *op. cit.* Also: "Psychical Hermaphrodism and the Masculine Protest" (*IP*, 16-22).

8. The best study of the mytheme from the perspective of depth psychopathology is that by Rafael Lopez-Pedraza, *Hermes and his Children*, (Zurich: Spring Publ. 1977), esp. Chap I, on Hermaphroditus.

9. For a critique of oppositionalism in psychology see my *The Dream and the Underworld*, (N. Y.: Harper & Row, 1979); for two examples of syzygy consciousness see my "Senex and Puer," in *Puer Papers* (Dallas: Spring Publ., 1979) and "Anima II" pp. 138-145.

10. The most fundamental literalism in Adler is the gender pair, male-female, "the only real antithesis" (NC 99) to which all others can be reduced. On the relation of literalism and gender-thinking, see P. Berry, "The Dogma of Gender," in her *Echo's Subtle Body* (Dallas:

Spring Publ., 1982). My view of Adler's male-female antithesis is that this syzygy stands for another basic metaphorical pair, spirit/soul, which cannot be taken literally in the same empirical and concrete manner as male and female.

11. R. I. Huber, "Social Interest Revisited," *Character Potential* 7, 1975, pp. 69f.

12. Note here the difference between Jung's frequent stress on meaning as something one searches for, or integrates as one realizes the Self, and Adler's statement that meanings are already there, that we live in the midst of meanings. Where Jung's sense of meaning is prophetic and religious, Adler's is interpretive and pragmatic.

12a. Cf. Gregory Bateson (ed.), *Perceval's Narrative*, (Stanford Univ. Press, 1961), for an early nineteenth-century witness of an incarcerated 'madman' who attributes his period of insanity to having taken 'literally' the speech of the spirit.

13. E.g. G. J. Mozdzierz, F. J. Macchitelli, & J. Lisiecki, "The Paradox in Psychotherapy: An Adlerian Perspective," *J. Indiv. Psychol.* 32/2, 1976, pp. 169-184; O'C '77.

14. "Junktim: purposive connection of two thoughts and affect-complexes that have in reality little or nothing to do with one another, in order to strengthen the affect. The metaphor has a similar origin" (*IP*, 39n, cf. A & A, 283). Adler's *junktim* compares with Jung's *complex*. Both terms are also akin in the construction of their meaning to the Greek *symptoma*, a chance falling together. Jung takes the complex objectively. It is a basic datum of the psyche, presenting the *empirical contents of its affects*, and so complexes can be demonstrated by means of the association experiment. Adler, however, takes the junktim as a purposive *invention to intensify affects*, much like the rhetoric of hyperbole and condensation in dreams and poetry (*L*, 79; *U*, 116; *IP*, 219n; A&A, 360-361). If we now combine complex and junktim we may understand our complexes both as empirical facts that are the nuclei of our psychic energy and also as the metaphors of our psychic myths. Re-conceiving the complex as a verbal image (metaphor) shifts the basis of mind from scientific descriptions to poetic descriptions. Paul Kugler has begun this seismic move of shifting the scientistic bed-rock of Jungian empiricism by re-examining Jung's writings on word association for their linguistic and imagistic significance. Paul Kugler, *The Alchemy of Discourse*, (Lewisburg, Pa.: Bucknell Univ. Press). It is curious to find that Jung, in his 82nd year (Letter to Hanhart, *Briefe III*, hrsg. Jaffé & Adler, [Olten: Walter, 1973], p. 79) still retained memory of Adler's junktim, although Jung there uses it as a forerunner of his synchronicity concept (the falling together of causally unrelated events, *symptoma*). Freud spoke of a "Junktim zwischen Heilen und Forschen" in his late paper on Lay Analysis. The term itself in German has its usual home in legal-political contexts

15. *Waking Dreams*, (N. Y.: Harper Colophon, 1977).

16. *Power in the Helping Professions*, (Dallas: Spring Publications, 1979).

17. "Demeter/Persephone and Neurosis"*Spr* '75; "What's the Matter with Mother?" Guild of Pastoral Psychology, Pamphlet 1978; cf. "On Reduction" *Spr*'73 and "Radical Woman" Lecture given at Univ. Notre Dame, Annual Jung Conference, 1977. These papers by Berry are now in her *Echo's Subtle Body* (Dallas: Spring Publ., 1982).

18. "Archetypal Psychology and Education" Paper contributed to the First International Seminar on Archetypal Psychology, Univ. of Dallas, 1977.
19. Cf. *Eranos 44-1975, Eranos 46-1977, Eranos 50-1981*; also *Spring* '73, '76, '80; *Gods and Games*, (Cleveland: World, 1969).
20. Cf. Jung, CW 7, 339, and my discussion of the mistaken ways we can understand Jung's idea of "integrating the anima" in my article, "Anima (II)," *Spring* '74, pp. 119-124.
21. Cf. *U, 13, 27; L, 9* on the importance of mistakes, and the way of error as the only way of getting to know the soul and to find meaning.
22. C. G. Jung, *Briefe*, Bd. II, ed. G. Adler and A. Jaffe, (Olten/Freiburg: Walter, 1972), p. 188; also p. 225. On the relation of anima and psyche and the inner/outer problem, see my "Anima" *Spring* '73, pp. 119-130.
23. "Social feeling is perhaps the most difficult concept in Adler's psychology to grasp correctly. Its essence is missed if it is taken to be either a philosophy or a morality. 'If anyone talks to me of morality,' Adler once remarked, 'I look to see if perchance his hand is not in my pocket.' Psychology is not concerned...to moralize...its aim is therapeutic. Social feeling...is a basic assumption about life which a person must possess if he is to...retain his psychic good health" (W, 208-209).
24. For a detailed psychological interpretation of the metaphors of Eros' father and mother (derived from Plato's account in *Symposium* referred to in my motto to this chapter) see the Sears Jayne translation of *Commentary on Plato's "Symposium" on Love* by Marsilio Ficino, second edition, forthcoming Spring Publications, VI: 7.

Library of Congress Cataloging-in-Publication Data

Hillman, James.
  Healing fiction / James Hillman.
    p. cm.
  Originally published: Barrytown, N.Y. : Station Hill Press, c1983.
  Includes bibliographical references.
  ISBN 0-88214-363-8 (pbk. : acid-free paper)
  1. Psychoanalysis and literature. I. Title.
PN56.P92H5 1994
150.19'5—dc20   94-9422
                                        CIP

ALSO BY JAMES HILLMAN FROM SPRING PUBLICATIONS

Salt and the Alchemical Soul • C. G. Jung, James Hillman, and Ernest Jones
Edited with an introduction by Stanton Marlan

The image of salt has touched human behavior, feeling, and expression, from marriage rites and customs to economics, from fertility to friendship, from superstition to being the basic stuff of human life. Not surprisingly, salt has become a focus of depth psychology. *Salt and the Alchemical Soul* is a collection of three significant papers newly edited and introduced, providing excellent examples of different methods and styles of working with images. (176 pp.) ISBN 0-88214-222-4

Insearch: Psychology and Religion • James Hillman

Insearch has become one of the few enduring descriptions of Jungian therapy in its relation to religion. Hillman's four chapters—the Human Encounter, the Unconscious as Experience, the Inner Morality of the Shadow, and the Inner Feminine or Anima—give a comprehensive account of Jungian psychology from the inside. His examples are fresh, his language easy, and the evident pleasure he takes in opening the great questions of the soul make this book a basic teaching text, an introduction to psychotherapy, and a consistently quoted reference for pastoral counseling. Includes a new preface by the author. (141 pp.) ISBN 0-88214-512-6

Oedipus Variations • Karl Kerényi and James Hillman

Kerényi elucidates both the ancient Oedipus myth—red-haired temper, swollen feet, and crossroads—and dramatic versions from Seneca to Eliot. Hillman inverts the emphasis of Father Freud's famous complex: why do fathers kill their sons? He shows that, in addition to the curse, murder, incest, and disease, the myth contains beauty, blessing, love, and loyalty. (170 pp.) ISBN 0-88214-219-4
(Available from Spring Audio: Hillman's *The Death of Oedipus* tape.)

Inter Views
Conversations on Psychotherapy, Biography, Love, Soul, Dreams, Work, Imagination
James Hillman with Laura Pozzo

This is the only biography of Hillman that he will let you read. Extraordinary yet practical accounts of active imagination, writing, daily work, and symptoms in their relation to love. William Kotzwinkle, author of the movie classic E. T., writes: "*Inter Views* is a lens focused by the bright gods, the archetypes, with whom Hillman is in creative rapport." (198 pp.) ISBN 0-88214-348-4

Suicide and the Soul • James Hillman

Is suicide ever justified by the soul? What is the basis for suicide being illegal and anathema to medicine? This early work of Hillman's examines the differences between the medical model of therapy and one that engages soul. Since the book's publication in 1964, it has enjoyed wide recognition in many languages and as a teaching text. (191 pp.) ISBN 0-88214-208-9

The Thought of the Heart and the Soul of the World • James Hillman

Two pivotal essays move archetypal psychology more into the world. Once the heart is no longer seen as just a pump or as the seat of personal feelings, it reclaims its place as an organ of aesthetics, responding to the world's beauty. Social and environmental catastrophes witness the world's suffering and appeal to us to attend to its soul. (130 pp.) ISBN 0-88214-353-0

For a free catalog, write:
Spring Publications, Inc.
299 East Quassett Road, Woodstock, CT 06281
tel: (860)974-3428